BRANDEE JANKOSKI and KEVIN GLYNN

Sauces, Rubs and Marinades

Versatile Flavors Beyond the Grill Includes Over
100 Rubs, Marinades, Salsas, Sauces, Reductions
and More

This book was professionally typeset on Reedsy.
Find out more at reedsy.com

Contents

4 Perfecting Marinades 53

Marinade Recipes

5 Elevating Sauces 100

1
Introduction

The world of culinary delights is a vast and exciting one, where the art of cooking transcends mere sustenance and enters the realm of sensory pleasure. At the heart of this culinary magic lie the secrets of rubs, marinades, and sauces, three elements that have the power to transform a simple meal into an unforgettable dining experience.

Imagine savoring a perfectly grilled steak, its exterior seared to a mouthwatering crust, and its interior bursting with juices that hint at a symphony of flavors. Picture a tender, marinated chicken, infused with herbs and spices that transport your taste buds to far-off lands. Visualize a plate adorned with delicate vegetables, bathed in a velvety sauce that adds depth and character to each bite. These are the moments that elevate cooking from a chore to an art form, and they all start with the careful selection and skillful application of rubs, marinades, and sauces.

In "Savor the Flavor: A Comprehensive Guide to Rubs, Marinades, and Sauces," we embark on a culinary journey that will not only enhance your cooking skills but also awaken your palate to a world of possibilities. Whether you are a novice in the kitchen or an experienced chef, this book is designed to inspire, educate, and ignite your passion for culinary exploration.

In the pages that follow, we will delve into the fundamentals of rubs, marinades, and sauces, demystifying their differences and teaching you the techniques to master them. From the simplest dry rubs to complex, multi-layered sauces, you'll discover the art of balancing flavors, textures, and aromas to create dishes that will leave a lasting impression on your guests.

We will explore the creative process of crafting your own signature rubs, marinades, and sauces, allowing you to customize your cooking to your unique tastes and preferences. Along the way, you'll learn how to pair and complement flavors, experiment with international and regional influences, and adapt to various dietary requirements, making you a versatile and confident cook.

But this book is more than just a collection of recipes and cooking tips; it is an invitation to embark on a flavorful adventure. It's a celebration of the joy that comes from creating memorable meals that nourish both body and soul. It's an opportunity to expand your culinary horizons, to explore new tastes and traditions, and to savor the flavors of the world from the comfort of your own kitchen.

So, whether you're planning a special occasion feast, a casual weeknight dinner, or simply seeking to elevate your everyday cooking, "Savor the Flavor" is your trusted companion on this gastronomic journey. Together, we'll unlock the secrets of rubs, marinades, and sauces, and by the end of this journey, you'll be well on your way to becoming a true flavor maestro.

Let's embark on this flavorful adventure together and discover the endless possibilities that await us in the world of rubs, marinades, and sauces. Your culinary masterpiece is just a few pages away.

The Art of Enhancing Flavor:

At its core, cooking is an art form that engages all our senses. From the sizzle of a hot skillet to the vibrant colors of fresh produce, the tactile sensation of kneading dough to the enticing aroma of a simmering pot, every aspect of the culinary experience contributes to the pleasure of eating. However, the most profound and memorable element of this sensory symphony is undoubtedly the flavor.

Flavor is the soul of every dish, the essence that lingers on our taste buds, and the memory that stays with us long after the meal has ended. It is the reason why we return to our favorite restaurants, the motivation behind our culinary adventures, and the secret ingredient that transforms humble ingredients into extraordinary creations.

The art of enhancing flavor is the heart of cooking. It involves the skillful manipulation of ingredients, techniques, and seasonings to create a harmo- nious and balanced taste experience. Rubs, marinades, and sauces are the tools in a chef's arsenal that enable them to craft layers of flavor, adding depth, complexity, and excitement to every bite.

Understanding the intricacies of flavor is essential for any aspiring chef. It involves recognizing the five primary taste sensations: sweet, sour, salty, bitter, and umami. Each of these tastes plays a role in the overall flavor profile of a dish, and mastering their interplay is the key to culinary excellence.

- Sweetness: Often associated with sugars, sweetness can come from a variety of sources, including fruits, vegetables, and even certain spices. It balances out the other tastes, providing a pleasant contrast to saltiness, sourness, and bitterness.

- Sourness: Sourness adds brightness and freshness to a dish. It can be derived from ingredients like citrus fruits, vinegar, or fermented foods. Sour elements awaken the palate and can cut through richness.

- Saltiness: Salt is a universal flavor enhancer. It not only makes food taste more savory but also heightens the perception of other flavors. Used judiciously, salt can be a chef's best friend.

- Bitterness: Bitterness, often found in ingredients like dark greens, coffee, and certain spices, adds complexity to a dish. When balanced correctly, bitterness can be a pleasant and intriguing aspect of the flavor profile.

- Umami: Umami is the elusive fifth taste, characterized by a savory and meaty quality. It can be found in foods like mushrooms, tomatoes, aged cheeses, and soy sauce. Umami enhances depth and richness in dishes.

In addition to these primary tastes, aroma also plays a crucial role in flavor perception. Our sense of smell is intimately connected to our sense of taste, and the aroma of a dish can greatly influence our perception of its flavor. This is why a well-seasoned pot of soup can be so comforting or why the scent of fresh-baked bread can be so inviting.

Rubs, marinades, and sauces are the vehicles through which we introduce these flavors and aromas to our dishes. They are the means by which we build layers of taste, infuse ingredients with character, and create well-balanced and memorable meals. Whether you're grilling a steak, roasting vegetables, or simmering a stew, the art of enhancing flavor is your guide to creating culinary masterpieces that delight the senses and nourish the soul.

In the chapters that follow, we will explore the nuances of rubs, marinades, and sauces, learning how to harness the power of ingredients, techniques, and creativity to elevate your cooking to new heights. So, prepare to embark on a flavorful journey, where each page brings you closer to becoming a true flavor maestro.

The Importance of Rubs, Marinades, and Sauces:

Rubs, marinades, and sauces are the unsung heroes of the culinary world, quietly working their magic to elevate dishes from ordinary to extraordinary. They are the key to transforming raw ingredients into flavorful, mouthwater- ing creations that leave a lasting impression. But what makes these elements so essential to the art of cooking?

1. Flavor Enhancement: Perhaps the most obvious role of rubs, marinades, and sauces is to enhance flavor. They infuse ingredients with a myriad of tastes and aromas, turning a bland piece of meat or a simple vegetable into a tantalizing symphony of flavors. Whether it's a smoky barbecue rub, a zesty citrus marinade, or a velvety mushroom sauce, these culinary tools

have the power to make your taste buds dance with delight.

2. Moisture and Tenderness: Marinades are renowned for their ability to tenderize meat by breaking down tough fibers, making it more succulent and enjoyable to eat. Additionally, they help retain moisture during cooking, preventing dryness and ensuring a juicy and tender result. Rubs, when applied correctly, can create a flavorful crust that seals in moisture, while sauces can add a final layer of moisture and richness.

3. Versatility: Rubs, marinades, and sauces are incredibly versatile. They can be customized to suit various ingredients and cooking methods, making them suitable for a wide range of culinary endeavors. Whether you're grilling, roasting, frying, or simmering, there's a rub, marinade, or sauce that can enhance your dish.

4. Creativity and Personalization: These flavor-enhancing elements offer endless opportunities for creativity in the kitchen. You can experiment with different ingredients, proportions, and techniques to create your own signature rubs, marinades, and sauces. This allows you to tailor your dishes to your personal taste preferences and culinary style.

5. Cultural and Regional Influence: Rubs, marinades, and sauces also serve as a gateway to exploring the diverse and rich culinary traditions from around the world. They provide a window into the flavors of different cultures and regions, allowing you to embark on a gastronomic journey without leaving your kitchen.

6. Elevating Everyday Cooking: While rubs, marinades, and sauces are often associated with special occasions and gourmet dishes, they can also elevate everyday cooking. With a well-stocked pantry and some creativity, you can turn weeknight meals into culinary adventures, bringing excitement and variety to your daily menu.

In the pages that follow, we will dive deeper into each of these aspects, unveiling the secrets of rubs, marinades, and sauces and showcasing their indispensable role in the world of cooking.

2

Understanding the Basics

The Difference Between Rubs, Marinades, and Sauces:

In the world of culinary arts, rubs, marinades, and sauces are the pillars upon which flavor is built. Understanding the distinctions between these fundamental elements is crucial for any aspiring chef. In this chapter, we'll unravel the mysteries of rubs, marinades, and sauces and explore when and how to use each of them.

1. Rubs:

- Definition: A rub is a mixture of dry ingredients, such as spices, herbs, salt, and sugar, that is applied to the surface of meat, poultry, seafood, or vegetables before cooking.

- Purpose: Rubs primarily enhance the exterior flavor and texture of dishes. They can create a flavorful crust or bark when grilled or roasted, adding depth and complexity.

- Application: Rubs are typically patted or massaged onto the food's surface, adhering to moisture on the surface. They can be used immediately before cooking or applied in advance for a more intense flavor.

-

1. Marinades:

- Definition: A marinade is a liquid mixture consisting of acidic and flavorful ingredients, such as vinegar, citrus juice, oil, herbs, spices, and sometimes sweeteners. Ingredients are soaked in the marinade for a specific period before cooking.

- Purpose: Marinades serve several functions. They tenderize proteins by breaking down muscle fibers, infuse flavors throughout the ingredient, and often add moisture.

- Application: Ingredients are submerged in the marinade, usually in a sealable container or plastic bag, and left to marinate for a designated time. The duration depends on the ingredient and desired flavor.

1. Sauces:

- Definition: Sauces are liquid or semi-liquid preparations, often thickened, that are served alongside or atop dishes to add moisture, flavor, and complexity.

- Purpose: Sauces play a versatile role in cooking. They can enhance, complement, or contrast with the primary dish, adding richness, depth, or a burst of flavor.

- Application: Sauces are prepared separately and added to dishes before or after cooking, depending on the desired effect.

Key Ingredients and Tools:

Before diving into the world of rubs, marinades, and sauces, it's essential to acquaint yourself with the key ingredients and tools commonly used in their preparation. These ingredients and tools will serve as the building blocks of your culinary creations.

Ingredients:

1. Herbs and Spices: A wide variety of herbs and spices form the foundation of rubs, marinades, and sauces. Common choices include basil, thyme, oregano, paprika, cumin, coriander, garlic, ginger, and more. Experi- mentation with different combinations can yield unique flavor profiles.

2. Acids: Acids such as citrus juice (lemon, lime, orange), vinegar (white, red wine, balsamic), and yogurt can be used in marinades to add bright- ness, balance flavors, and tenderize proteins.

3. Oils: Oils, like olive oil, vegetable oil, or sesame oil, are often used in marinades and as a base for salad dressings or sauces. They help distribute flavors and provide a rich mouthfeel.

4. Sweeteners: Sweeteners such as sugar, honey, maple syrup, and mo- lasses can balance out the acidity and heat in rubs, marinades, and sauces, creating a harmonious flavor profile.

5. Salt: Salt is a crucial ingredient for enhancing and highlighting flavors. It also plays a role in preserving food and enhancing texture.

6. Aromatics: Ingredients like garlic, onions, shallots, and ginger are essential for adding depth and complexity to your culinary creations.

7. Liquids: Various liquids, including soy sauce, Worcestershire sauce, fish sauce, and broth, contribute unique flavors and umami to sauces and marinades.

Tools:

1. Mixing Bowls: Different-sized mixing bowls are essential for combining and marinating ingredients.

2. Measuring Spoons and Cups: Precise measurements are crucial when working with rubs, marinades, and sauces.

3. Whisk: A whisk is handy for emulsifying liquids and combining ingredi- ents in sauces and marinades.

4. Food Processor or Blender: These appliances are used for blending and pureeing ingredients to create smooth sauces and marinades.

5. Graters and Zesters: Graters and zesters help extract the aromatic oils and zest from citrus fruits and fresh spices.

6. Sealable Containers or Plastic Bags: These are essential for marinating ingredients, allowing them to absorb flavors evenly.

7. Grinder or Mortar and Pestle: Used to freshly grind whole spices for rubs and marinades, releasing their full flavor potential.

Balancing Flavors and Textures:

Achieving the perfect balance of flavors and textures is an art in itself. Whether you're creating a rub, marinade, or sauce, un- derstanding how to harmonize different taste sensations is essential for culinary success. Here are some principles to keep in mind:

1. Sweet and Sour: Sweetness can balance the tangy acidity of citrus or vinegar in marinades and sauces. Conversely, a touch of sourness can complement sweet dishes by cutting through richness.

2. Salt and Umami: Salt enhances the overall flavor of a dish and plays well with umami-rich ingredients like soy sauce, mushrooms, or Parmesan cheese.

3. Heat and Spice: Spices and chili peppers can add heat and spice to your creations. Be mindful of their intensity and adjust quantities to your desired level of heat.

4. Texture: In sauces, consider how different textures can enhance a dish. Creamy, velvety sauces can complement crispy or grilled textures, while chunky sauces may pair well with tender meats.

5. Balance with Acid: The acidity from ingredients like vinegar or citrus can brighten and balance the richness of sauces and marinades.

As you venture further into the world of rubs, marinades, and sauces, you'll discover the art of fine-tuning flavors and textures to create dishes that are both satisfying and memorable. This understanding lays the foundation for your culinary journey, enabling you to experiment with confidence and creativity as you explore the chapters to come.

3
Mastering Rub_s

What Is a Rub?

A rub is a culinary concoction of dry ingredients that can turn a bland piece of meat, poultry, seafood, or even vegetables into a flavor-packed masterpiece. Unlike marinades and sauces, rubs are applied directly to the surface of the food and consist of a mixture of spices, herbs, salt, sugar, and sometimes other flavor enhancers. When used correctly, rubs create a delightful crust or bark on the exterior of the food during cooking, adding layers of complexity and a satisfying texture to every bite.

Characteristics of Rubs:

1. Dry Ingredients: Rubs are primarily composed of dry ingredients, such as ground spices, herbs, and seasonings.

2. Texture: Rubs have a grainy or powdery texture, which adheres to the food's surface and forms a flavorful coating.

3. Flavor Concentration: Since rubs are not diluted with liquid, their flavors are highly concentrated, which makes them excellent for enhancing the exterior taste of dishes.

4. Crust Formation: Rubs create a flavorful crust when exposed to high heat, sealing in moisture and infusing the food with intense flavor.

5. Versatility: Rubs can be customized to suit various flavor profiles, from spicy and smoky to sweet and savory, making them adaptable to different cuisines and dishes.

B. Dry Rub vs. Wet Rub:

When it comes to rubs, there are two primary categories: dry rubs and wet rubs. Each offers a distinct approach to enhancing flavor, and choosing the right one depends on your culinary goals and personal preferences.

1. Dry Rubs:

- Composition: Dry rubs consist solely of dry ingredients, such as spices, herbs, salt, and sugar.

- Texture: They have a powdery texture that adheres to the food's surface.

- Application: Dry rubs are applied directly to the dry surface of the food, adhering to it through moisture or oil present on the food's surface.

- Flavor Profile: Dry rubs create a concentrated burst of flavor on the exterior of the dish, forming a flavorful crust during cooking.

1. Wet Rubs:

- Composition: Wet rubs incorporate liquid components, such as oil, vinegar, or citrus juice, into the mix of dry ingredients.

- Texture: They have a paste-like consistency, making them adhere more easily to the food.

- Application: Wet rubs are spread directly onto the food's surface, forming a flavorful paste that clings to it.

- Flavor Profile: Wet rubs provide a moist and aromatic layer of flavor, enhancing the food's interior as well as its exterior. The liquid components can also act as a tenderizing agent.

C. Creating Your Signature Rub:

One of the joys of mastering rubs is the opportunity to craft your own signature blends, tailored to your unique taste preferences. Creating a signature rub involves experimentation and understanding the balance of flavors. Here's a step-by-step guide to help you get started:

1. Choose Your Base: Start with a base of salt, which is essential for enhancing flavor and drawing out moisture from the food. You can use kosher salt, sea salt, or specialty salts for a unique touch.

2. Select Aromatic Ingredients: Build the flavor profile by selecting a combination of aromatic ingredients. This can include spices like paprika, cumin, coriander, or cinnamon, as well as herbs like thyme, rosemary, oregano, or basil.

3. Add Heat and Depth: If you like spicy rubs, incorporate ingredients like chili powder, cayenne pepper, black pepper, or smoked paprika to add heat and depth.

4. Balancing Act: Achieve balance by adding sweet elements such as brown sugar, granulated sugar, or honey to counter-balance the saltiness and heat.

5. Experiment: Don't be afraid to experiment with various flavor compo- nents like garlic powder, onion powder, citrus zest, or even dried fruit for a unique twist.

6. Taste and Adjust: As you mix your rub, taste it periodically to ensure that it aligns with your flavor preferences. Adjust the ratios of ingredients as needed to create the perfect balance.

7. Keep Records: Once you've perfected your signature rub, make note of the ingredients and their proportions for future use. This way, you can recreate your masterpiece whenever you desire.

D. Application Techniques:

Applying a rub effectively is key to ensuring that it imparts maximum flavor to your dishes. The method of application depends on the type of food you're seasoning:

1. Meats: For meats like steak, chicken, pork, or lamb, generously coat the entire surface with the rub. Press it into the meat to ensure adherence. Allow the meat to rest for at least 30 minutes to let the flavors penetrate before cooking.

2. Seafood: Rubs can also enhance the flavor of seafood. Simply sprinkle or pat the rub onto the seafood, ensuring an even distribution. Allow the seafood to rest for a brief period before cooking.

3. Vegetables: Rubs can add depth to roasted or grilled vegetables. Toss the vegetables in a bit of oil to create a moist surfa-ce, then sprinkle the rub evenly over them before cooking.

Rub Recipes

Classic BBQ Rub Recipe

Ingredients:

- 1/4 cup brown sugar
- 2 tablespoons paprika
- 1 tablespoon kosher salt
- 1 tablespoon black pepper
- 1 tablespoon chili powder
- 1 teaspoon garlic powder
- 1 teaspoon onion powder
- 1/2 teaspoon cayenne pepper (adjust to taste for spiciness)

Instructions:

1. In a mixing bowl, combine the brown sugar, paprika, kosher salt, black pepper, chili powder, garlic powder, onion powder, and cayenne pepper.

2. Stir the ingredients together until they are thoroughly blended, creating a flavorful Classic BBQ Rub.

3. Taste the rub and adjust the level of spiciness by adding more or less cayenne pepper to suit your preference.

4. Transfer the Classic BBQ Rub to an airtight container or a spice jar with a tight-fitting lid. Store it in a cool, dry place until ready to use.

Suggested Uses for Classic BBQ Rub:

1. Barbecue Ribs: Rub the Classic BBQ Rub generously onto pork ribs before slow-cooking or grilling. It imparts a sweet and smoky flavor to the ribs.

2. Pulled Pork: Apply the rub to pork shoulder or butt before slow-cooking or smoking. The flavors infuse into the meat, creating tender and flavorful pulled pork.

3. Barbecue Chicken: Coat chicken pieces or whole chickens with the rub before grilling or smoking. It adds a savory and slightly sweet note to the chicken.

4. Smoked Brisket: Use the rub as a dry rub for smoked brisket. Apply it to the meat before smoking for a classic barbecue flavor profile.

5. Grilled Corn: Sprinkle the Classic BBQ Rub over grilled corn on the cob for a tasty and smoky twist on a classic side dish.

The Classic BBQ Rub is a timeless seasoning blend that embodies the essence of classic barbecue flavors. It pairs exceptionally well with various grilled and smoked dishes, making it a go-to rub for barbecue enthusiasts. Enjoy experimenting with different meats and recipes to showcase the deliciousness of this classic rub.

Sweet BBQ Rub Recipe

Ingredients:

- 1/4 cup brown sugar
- 2 tablespoons paprika
- 1 tablespoon chili powder
- 1 tablespoon garlic powder
- 1 tablespoon onion powder
- 1 tablespoon ground black pepper
- 1 tablespoon kosher salt
- 1 teaspoon cayenne pepper (adjust to taste for spiciness)

Instructions:

1. In a mixing bowl, combine the brown sugar, paprika, chili powder, garlic powder, onion powder, ground black pepper, kosher salt, and cayenne pepper (adjust to taste).

2. Stir the ingredients together until they are well blended, creating a flavorful Sweet BBQ Rub.

3. Taste the rub and adjust the level of spiciness or sweetness by adding more cayenne pepper or brown sugar to suit your preference.

4. Transfer the Sweet BBQ Rub to an airtight container or a spice jar with a tight-fitting lid. Store it in a cool, dry place until ready to use.

Suggested Uses for Sweet BBQ Rub:

1. Sweet BBQ Ribs: Rub the Sweet BBQ Rub onto ribs before slow-cooking or grilling for tender and flavorful ribs.

2. Sweet BBQ Pulled Pork: Season pork shoulder or butt with the rub before slow-cooking for delicious pulled pork sandwiches.

3. Sweet BBQ Chicken Wings: Coat chicken wings with the rub before baking or grilling for a sweet and savory appetizer.

4. Sweet BBQ Grilled Vegetables: Toss vegetables like corn, bell peppers, and zucchini in the rub before grilling for a sweet and smoky side dish.

5. Sweet BBQ Baked Beans: Add the rub to a pot of baked beans for a sweet and smoky twist on a classic side dish.

The Sweet BBQ Rub combines the sweetness of brown sugar with a blend of savory and smoky spices. It's a versatile seasoning blend that adds a delightful combination of sweet and savory flavors to your barbecue dishes. Enjoy experimenting with different recipes to showcase the deliciousness of this flavorful rub.

Cajun Rub Recipe

Ingredients:

- 2 tablespoons paprika

- 1 tablespoon garlic powder

- 1 tablespoon onion powder

- 1 tablespoon dried oregano

- 1 tablespoon dried thyme

- 1 teaspoon cayenne pepper (adjust to taste for spiciness)

- 1 teaspoon black pepper

- 1 teaspoon white pepper

- 1 teaspoon kosher salt

Instructions:

1.   In a mixing bowl, combine the paprika, garlic powder, onion powder, dried oregano, dried thyme, cayenne pepper, black pepper, white pepper, and kosher salt.

2.   Stir the ingredients together until they are well blended, creating a flavorful Cajun Rub.

3.   Taste the rub and adjust the level of spiciness by adding more or less cayenne pepper to suit your preference.

4.   Transfer the Cajun Rub to an airtight container or a spice jar with a tight- fitting lid. Store it in a cool, dry place until ready to use.

Suggested Uses for Cajun Rub:

1.   Cajun Grilled Shrimp: Coat shrimp with the Cajun Rub before grilling for a spicy and flavorful seafood dish.

2.   Cajun Grilled Chicken: Rub chicken pieces or whole chicken with the Cajun Rub before grilling or roasting for a zesty and savory flavor.

3.   Cajun Blackened Fish: Sprinkle the rub onto fish fillets (such as catfish or redfish) before blackening them in a hot skillet. It creates a spicy and flavorful crust.

4.   Cajun Roasted Vegetables: Toss vegetables like bell peppers, onions, and okra in the Cajun Rub before roasting for a Cajun-inspired side dish.

5.   Cajun Jambalaya: Use the rub as a seasoning for traditional Cajun jambalaya, adding it to rice, sausage, chicken, and shrimp for a classic Louisiana dish.

The Cajun Rub is a bold and spicy seasoning blend that captures the essence of Cajun cuisine. It adds a kick of flavor to various dishes, especially those with a Louisiana-inspired flair. Enjoy exploring the world of Cajun cooking with this delicious and versatile rub.

Lemon Herb Rub Recipe

Ingredients:

- 2 tablespoons dried thyme
- 2 tablespoons dried rosemary
- 2 tablespoons dried oregano
- Zest of 1 lemon
- 2 cloves garlic, minced
- 1 teaspoon kosher salt
- 1 teaspoon black pepper
- 1/2 teaspoon red pepper flakes (adjust to taste)

Instructions:

1.   In a mixing bowl, combine the dried thyme, dried rosemary, dried oregano, lemon zest, minced garlic, kosher salt, black pepper, and red pepper flakes.

2.   Stir the ingredients together until they are well blended, creating a fragrant Lemon Herb Rub.

3.   Taste the rub and adjust the level of spiciness by adding more or less red pepper flakes to suit your preference.

4.   Transfer the Lemon Herb Rub to an airtight container or a spice jar with a tight-fitting lid. Store it in a cool, dry place until ready to use.

Suggested Uses for Lemon Herb Rub:

1.   Grilled Chicken: Rub chicken pieces or whole chickens with the Lemon Herb Rub before grilling or roasting. The lemon and herb flavors create a bright and aromatic dish.

2.   Lemon Herb Salmon: Coat salmon fillets with the rub before grilling or baking. It pairs perfectly with the rich flavors of salmon.

3.   Lemon Herb Roasted Vegetables: Toss a variety of vegetables (such as potatoes, carrots, and bell peppers) in the Lemon Herb Rub before roasting for a fragrant and herbaceous side dish.

4.   Lemon Herb Pasta: Sprinkle the rub over freshly cooked pasta and mix it with olive oil for a simple yet flavorful pasta dish. Add grated Parmesan cheese for extra richness.

5.   Lemon Herb Marinade: Combine the rub with olive oil and lemon juice to create a marinade for poultry, fish, or vegetables. Let the ingredients meld for at least 30 minutes before cooking.

The Lemon Herb Rub is a versatile seasoning blend that brightens up dishes with its zesty lemon and aromatic herbaceous notes. It's perfect for grilling, roasting, and marinating a variety of ingredients, adding a burst of fresh flavor to your meals. Enjoy exploring different culinary creations with this delightful rub.

Smoky Chipotle Rub Recipe

Ingredients:

· 2 tablespoons smoked paprika

· 2 tablespoons chipotle powder (adjust to taste for spiciness)

· 1 tablespoon brown sugar

· 1 tablespoon garlic powder

· 1 tablespoon onion powder

· 1 teaspoon ground cumin

· 1 teaspoon dried oregano

· 1 teaspoon kosher salt

· 1/2 teaspoon black pepper

Instructions:

1.   In a mixing bowl, combine the smoked paprika, chipotle powder, brown sugar, garlic powder, onion powder, ground cumin, dried oregano, kosher salt, and black pepper.

2.   Stir the ingredients together until they are well blended, creating a flavorful Smoky Chipotle Rub.

3.   Taste the rub and adjust the level of spiciness by adding more or less chipotle powder to suit your preference.

4.   Transfer the Smoky Chipotle Rub to an airtight container or a spice jar with a tight-fitting lid. Store it in a cool, dry place until ready to use.

Suggested Uses for Smoky Chipotle Rub:

1.   Smoky Chipotle BBQ Ribs: Rub the Smoky Chipotle Rub generously onto pork ribs before slow-cooking or grilling. It imparts a smoky and spicy flavor to the ribs.

2.   Chipotle Grilled Chicken: Coat chicken pieces or whole chicken with the rub before grilling for a smoky and spicy kick.

3.   Smoky Chipotle Beef: Use the rub as a seasoning for beef steaks, burgers, or skewers before grilling. It adds a bold and smoky flavor to the meat.

4.   Smoky Chipotle Roasted Vegetables: Toss vegetables like sweet potatoes, Brussels sprouts, and red onions in the Smoky Chipotle Rub before roasting for a smoky and spicy side dish.

5.   Chipotle Seasoned Fries: Sprinkle the rub over freshly baked or fried potato wedges for a smoky and spicy twist on classic fries.

The Smoky Chipotle Rub is a bold and smoky seasoning blend that adds depth and heat to various grilled and roasted dishes. Its smoky chipotle flavor is perfect for those who enjoy a touch of smokiness and spiciness in their meals. Enjoy experimenting with different meats and vegetables to showcase the deliciousness of this flavorful rub.

Mediterranean Za'atar Rub Recipe

Ingredients:

·   2 tablespoons dried thyme

·   2 tablespoons sesame seeds

·   1 tablespoon dried oregano

·   1 tablespoon ground sumac

·   1 teaspoon ground cumin

·   1 teaspoon kosher salt

·   1/2 teaspoon black pepper

·   2 cloves garlic, minced

·   Zest of 1 lemon

Instructions:

1.   In a mixing bowl, combine the dried thyme, sesame seeds, dried oregano, ground sumac, ground cumin, kosher salt, black pepper, minced garlic, and lemon zest.

2.   Stir the ingredients together until they are well blended, creating a fragrant Mediterranean Za'atar Rub.

3.   Taste the rub and adjust the seasoning to your preference by adding more salt or black pepper if needed.

4.   Transfer the Mediterranean Za'atar Rub to an airtight container or a spice jar with a tight-fitting lid. Store it in a cool, dry place until ready to use.

Suggested Uses for Mediterranean Za'atar Rub:

1.   Za'atar Grilled Chicken: Rub chicken pieces or whole chickens with the Mediterranean Za'atar Rub before grilling or

roasting. It imparts a fragrant and savory flavor.

2.	Za'atar Roasted Vegetables: Toss vegetables like eggplant, zucchini, and cherry tomatoes in the Za'atar Rub before roasting for a Mediterranean- inspired side dish.

3.	Za'atar Hummus: Sprinkle the rub over a bowl of hummus for a flavorful garnish. Serve it with pita bread or fresh vegetables.

4.	Za'atar Flatbreads: Use the rub as a topping for homemade flatbreads or pizzas. Brush the dough with olive oil, sprinkle with the rub, and bake until golden and fragrant.

5.	Za'atar Yogurt Dip: Mix the rub into Greek yogurt for a simple and tasty dip. It's great for dipping pita chips, cucumber slices, or carrot sticks.

The Mediterranean Za'atar Rub is a versatile seasoning blend that captures the essence of Mediterranean cuisine with its aromatic herbs and sesame seeds. It adds depth and flavor to a variety of dishes, making it a delightful addition to your culinary repertoire. Enjoy exploring different Mediterranean-inspired creations with this fragrant rub.

Asian Five-Spice Rub Recipe

Ingredients:

·	1 tablespoon Chinese five-spice powder

·	1 tablespoon brown sugar

·	1 teaspoon ground ginger

·	1 teaspoon garlic powder

·	1/2 teaspoon ground cinnamon

·	1/2 teaspoon ground star anise (optional, for extra depth)

·	1/2 teaspoon kosher salt

·	1/4 teaspoon black pepper

Instructions:

1.	In a mixing bowl, combine the Chinese five-spice powder, brown sugar, ground ginger, garlic powder, ground cinnamon, ground star anise (if using), kosher salt, and black pepper.

2.	Stir the ingredients together until they are well blended, creating a flavorful Asian Five-Spice Rub.

3.	Taste the rub and adjust the seasoning to your preference by adding more brown sugar for sweetness or more salt for saltiness.

4.	Transfer the Asian Five-Spice Rub to an airtight container or a spice jar with a tight-fitting lid. Store it in a cool, dry place until ready to use.

Suggested Uses for Asian Five-Spice Rub:

1.   Five-Spice Grilled Chicken: Rub chicken pieces or whole chickens with the Asian Five-Spice Rub before grilling or roasting. It imparts a fragrant and savory flavor with a touch of sweetness.

2.   Five-Spice Pork Tenderloin: Coat pork tenderloin with the rub before grilling or roasting for a delicious and aromatic dish.

3.   Five-Spice Roasted Vegetables: Toss vegetables like sweet potatoes, carrots, and broccoli in the Five-Spice Rub before roasting for a unique and flavorful side dish.

4.   Five-Spice Stir-Fry: Use the rub as a seasoning for stir-fry dishes. It adds depth of flavor to a variety of vegetables and proteins.

5.   Five-Spice Glaze: Mix the rub with honey, soy sauce, and a splash of rice vinegar to create a sweet and savory glaze for grilled or roasted meats.

The Asian Five-Spice Rub is a versatile seasoning blend that combines the aromatic flavors of Chinese cuisine. It adds a distinctive and complex flavor profile to a variety of dishes, making it a delightful addition to your culinary creations. Enjoy exploring different Asian-inspired recipes with this fragrant rub.

Herb and Mustard Rub Recipe

Ingredients:

- 2 tablespoons dried thyme
- 2 tablespoons dried rosemary
- 1 tablespoon dried sage
- 1 tablespoon dried oregano
- 1 tablespoon dried basil
- 2 tablespoons yellow mustard seeds
- 2 teaspoons kosher salt
- 1 teaspoon black pepper
- 2 cloves garlic, minced

Instructions:

1.   In a mixing bowl, combine the dried thyme, dried rosemary, dried sage, dried oregano, dried basil, yellow mustard seeds, kosher salt, black pepper, and minced garlic.

2.   Stir the ingredients together until they are well blended, creating a flavorful Herb and Mustard Rub.

3.	Taste the rub and adjust the seasoning to your preference by adding more salt or black pepper if needed.

4.	Transfer the Herb and Mustard Rub to an airtight container or a spice jar with a tight-fitting lid. Store it in a cool, dry place until ready to use.

Suggested Uses for Herb and Mustard Rub:

1.	Herb and Mustard Grilled Chicken: Rub chicken pieces or whole chickens with the Herb and Mustard Rub before grilling or roasting. The combina- tion of herbs and mustard seeds creates a savory and aromatic flavor.

2.	Herb and Mustard Pork Chops: Coat pork chops with the rub before grilling or pan-searing. It adds a flavorful and slightly tangy note to the pork.

3.	Herb and Mustard Roasted Potatoes: Toss potato wedges or cubes in the Herb and Mustard Rub before roasting for a fragrant and herbaceous side dish.

4.	Herb and Mustard Marinade: Mix the rub with olive oil and a splash of white wine vinegar to create a flavorful marinade for poultry or pork. Allow the ingredients to meld for at least 30 minutes before cooking.

5.	Herb and Mustard Salad Dressing: Combine the rub with olive oil, red wine vinegar, and a touch of honey to create a tasty salad dressing with a hint of herbs and mustard.

The Herb and Mustard Rub is a versatile seasoning blend that combines the savory flavors of herbs with the zesty kick of mustard seeds. It enhances the taste of a variety of meats, vegetables, and dressings, making it a wonderful addition to your culinary reper- toire. Enjoy experimenting with different recipes to showcase the deliciousness of this aromatic rub.

Coffee and Cocoa Rub Recipe

Ingredients:

·	2 tablespoons finely ground coffee beans

·	2 tablespoons unsweetened cocoa powder

·	2 tablespoons brown sugar

·	1 tablespoon smoked paprika

·	1 teaspoon chili powder

·	1 teaspoon kosher salt

·	1/2 teaspoon black pepper

·	1/2 teaspoon garlic powder

Instructions:

1.   In a mixing bowl, combine the finely ground coffee beans, unsweetened cocoa powder, brown sugar, smoked paprika, chili powder, kosher salt, black pepper, and garlic powder.

2.   Stir the ingredients together until they are well blended, creating a flavorful Coffee and Cocoa Rub.

3.   Taste the rub and adjust the level of sweetness or spiciness by adding more brown sugar or chili powder to suit your preference.

4.   Transfer the Coffee and Cocoa Rub to an airtight container or a spice jar with a tight-fitting lid. Store it in a cool, dry place until ready to use.

Suggested Uses for Coffee and Cocoa Rub:

1.   Coffee and Cocoa Grilled Steak: Rub steak cuts with the Coffee and Cocoa Rub before grilling. The combination of coffee and cocoa enhances the richness of the meat.

2.   Coffee and Cocoa Pork Ribs: Apply the rub to pork ribs before slow- cooking or grilling for a smoky and slightly sweet flavor.

3.   Coffee and Cocoa Chicken Wings: Coat chicken wings with the rub before baking or grilling for a unique and flavorful twist on classic wings.

4.   Coffee and Cocoa Roasted Vegetables: Toss vegetables like butternut squash, Brussels sprouts, and carrots in the Coffee and Cocoa Rub before roasting for a sweet and smoky side dish.

5.   Coffee and Cocoa Dry Rub: Use the rub as a dry rub for various meats, such as pork shoulder, brisket, or even tofu, before slow-cooking or smoking.

The Coffee and Cocoa Rub is a distinctive seasoning blend that combines the bold flavors of coffee and cocoa with smoky and savory elements. It adds a rich and aromatic profile to grilled, roasted, and slow-cooked dishes, making it a unique and delightful addition to your culinary repertoire. Enjoy experimenting with different recipes to showcase the deliciousness of this flavorful rub.

Italian Herb Rub Recipe

Ingredients:

·   2 tablespoons dried basil

·   2 tablespoons dried oregano

·   2 tablespoons dried thyme

·   1 tablespoon dried rosemary

·   1 tablespoon dried parsley

·   1 tablespoon garlic powder

·   1 teaspoon onion powder

·   1 teaspoon kosher salt

- 1/2 teaspoon black pepper
- 1/4 teaspoon red pepper flakes (adjust to taste for spiciness)

Instructions:

1.   In a mixing bowl, combine the dried basil, dried oregano, dried thyme, dried rosemary, dried parsley, garlic powder, onion powder, kosher salt, black pepper, and red pepper flakes (adjust to taste).

2.   Stir the ingredients together until they are well blended, creating a flavorful Italian Herb Rub.

3.   Taste the rub and adjust the level of spiciness by adding more or less red pepper flakes to suit your preference.

4.   Transfer the Italian Herb Rub to an airtight container or a spice jar with a tight-fitting lid. Store it in a cool, dry place until ready to use.

Suggested Uses for Italian Herb Rub:

1.   Italian Herb Grilled Chicken: Rub chicken pieces or whole chickens with the Italian Herb Rub before grilling or roasting. The blend of herbs creates a fragrant and savory flavor.

2.   Italian Herb Roasted Potatoes: Toss potato wedges or cubes in the rub before roasting for a flavorful and herbaceous side dish.

3.   Italian Herb Pasta Sauce: Add the rub to a homemade tomato sauce for pasta. Simmer to infuse the flavors before serving over your favorite pasta.

4.   Italian Herb Salad Dressing: Mix the rub with olive oil, red wine vinegar, and a touch of Dijon mustard to create a delicious Italian herb salad dressing.

5.   Italian Herb Focaccia: Sprinkle the rub over homemade or store-bought focaccia bread before baking for a fragrant and tasty bread.

The Italian Herb Rub is a versatile seasoning blend that captures the essence of Italian cuisine with its aromatic herbs and savory spices. It enhances the taste of a variety of dishes, making it a wonderful addition to your culinary repertoire. Enjoy experimenting with different Italian-inspired recipes to showcase the deliciousness of this fragrant rub.

Lavender and Honey Rub Recipe

Ingredients:

- 1 tablespoon dried culinary lavender buds
- 2 tablespoons honey (warmed for easy mixing)
- 2 tablespoons brown sugar
- 1 tablespoon dried rosemary
- 1 teaspoon dried thyme

- 1 teaspoon dried sage

- 1 teaspoon kosher salt

- 1/2 teaspoon black pepper

- Zest of 1 lemon

Instructions:

1.   In a mixing bowl, combine the dried culinary lavender buds, warmed honey, brown sugar, dried rosemary, dried thyme, dried sage, kosher salt, black pepper, and lemon zest.

2.   Stir the ingredients together until they are well blended, creating a fragrant Lavender and Honey Rub.

3.   Taste the rub and adjust the level of sweetness or herbal notes by adding more honey or lavender buds to suit your preference.

4.   Transfer the Lavender and Honey Rub to an airtight container or a spice jar with a tight-fitting lid. Store it in a cool, dry place until ready to use.

Suggested Uses for Lavender and Honey Rub:

1.   Lavender and Honey Grilled Chicken: Rub chicken pieces or whole chickens with the Lavender and Honey Rub before grilling or roasting. It imparts a fragrant and slightly sweet flavor.

2.   Lavender and Honey Glazed Pork: Use the rub as a dry rub for pork tenderloin or chops, then finish with a lavender and honey glaze during cooking.

3.   Lavender and Honey Roasted Vegetables: Toss a medley of root vegeta- bles, such as carrots, parsnips, and sweet potatoes, in the Lavender and Honey Rub before roasting for a unique and flavorful side dish.

4.   Lavender and Honey Salad Dressing: Combine the rub with olive oil, white wine vinegar, and a touch of Dijon mustard to create a delicate lavender and honey salad dressing.

5.   Lavender and Honey Marinade: Mix the rub with additional honey and lemon juice to create a marinade for chicken or pork. Allow the flavors to meld for at least 30 minutes before cooking.

The Lavender and Honey Rub is a distinctive and aromatic seasoning blend that combines the floral notes of lavender with the sweetness of honey. It adds a unique and delicate flavor profile to a variety of dishes, making it a delightful addition to your culinary repertoire. Enjoy experimenting with different recipes to showcase the deliciousness of this fragrant rub.

Blackened Cajun Rub Recipe

Ingredients:

- 2 tablespoons paprika

- 1 tablespoon garlic powder

- · 1 tablespoon onion powder

- · 1 tablespoon dried thyme

- · 1 tablespoon dried oregano

- · 1 tablespoon dried basil

- · 2 teaspoons cayenne pepper (adjust to taste for spiciness)

- · 11/2 teaspoons kosher salt

- · 11/2 teaspoons black pepper

- · 1 teaspoon white pepper (optional for extra heat)

Instructions:

1.   In a mixing bowl, combine the paprika, garlic powder, onion powder, dried thyme, dried oregano, dried basil, cayenne pepper (adjust to taste), kosher salt, black pepper, and white pepper (if using).

2.   Stir the ingredients together until they are well blended, creating a flavorful Blackened Cajun Rub.

3.   Taste the rub and adjust the level of spiciness by adding more or less cayenne pepper to suit your preference.

4.   Transfer the Blackened Cajun Rub to an airtight container or a spice jar with a tight-fitting lid. Store it in a cool, dry place until ready to use.

Suggested Uses for Blackened Cajun Rub:

1.   Blackened Cajun Chicken: Rub chicken pieces or chicken thighs with the Blackened Cajun Rub before grilling or pan--searing for a spicy and flavorful dish.

2.   Blackened Cajun Shrimp: Season shrimp with the rub before sautéing or grilling for a zesty and spicy seafood option.

3.   Blackened Cajun Catfish: Coat catfish fillets with the rub before pan- frying or baking for a Southern-inspired and spicy fish dish.

4.   Blackened Cajun Vegetables: Toss a mix of vegetables like bell peppers, okra, and corn in the rub before sautéing or roasting for a flavorful and spicy side dish.

5.   Blackened Cajun Pasta: Mix the rub with heavy cream and Parmesan cheese to create a spicy Cajun Alfredo sauce for pasta dishes.

The Blackened Cajun Rub is a bold and spicy seasoning blend that captures the essence of Cajun cuisine. It adds a rich and fiery flavor profile to a variety of dishes, making it a fantastic addition to your culinary repertoire. Enjoy experimenting with different Cajun-inspired recipes to showcase the deliciousness of this flavorful rub.

Berbere Spice Rub Recipe

Ingredients:

- 2 tablespoons ground paprika

- 1 tablespoon ground cayenne pepper (adjust to taste for spiciness)

- 1 tablespoon ground coriander

- 1 tablespoon ground cumin

- 1 tablespoon ground ginger

- 1 tablespoon ground cinnamon

- 1 teaspoon ground cardamom

- 1 teaspoon ground cloves

- 1 teaspoon ground allspice

- 1 teaspoon ground fenugreek

- 1/2 teaspoon ground nutmeg

- 1/2 teaspoon ground black pepper

- 1/2 teaspoon kosher salt

Instructions:

1.   In a mixing bowl, combine the ground paprika, ground cayenne pepper (adjust to taste), ground coriander, ground cumin, ground ginger, ground cinnamon, ground cardamom, ground cloves, ground allspice, ground fenugreek, ground nutmeg, ground black pepper, and kosher salt.

2.   Stir the ingredients together until they are well blended, creating a flavorful Berbere Spice Rub.

3.   Taste the rub and adjust the level of spiciness by adding more or less cayenne pepper to suit your preference.

4.   Transfer the Berbere Spice Rub to an airtight container or a spice jar with a tight-fitting lid. Store it in a cool, dry place until ready to use.

Suggested Uses for Berbere Spice Rub:

1.   Berbere Spice Grilled Chicken: Rub chicken pieces with the Berbere Spice Rub before grilling for a spicy and aromatic dish.

2.   Berbere Spice Roasted Vegetables: Toss a mix of vegetables like sweet potatoes, carrots, and cauliflower in the rub before roasting for a flavorful and spicy side dish.

3.   Berbere Spice Lentil Soup: Add the rub to a pot of lentil soup for an Ethiopian-inspired and spicy flavor.

4.   Berbere Spice Lamb Stew: Season lamb cubes with the rub before slow- cooking for a fragrant and hearty stew.

5.   Berbere Spice Rice Pilaf: Mix the rub with cooked rice, toasted nuts, and dried fruits for a fragrant and flavorful side dish.

The Berbere Spice Rub is a bold and spicy seasoning blend that captures the vibrant flavors of Ethiopian cuisine. It adds an exotic and aromatic touch to a variety of dishes, making it a delightful addition to your culinary repertoire. Enjoy experimenting with different recipes to showcase the deliciousness of this flavorful rub.

Caribbean Jerk Rub Recipe

Ingredients:

- 2 tablespoons ground allspice
- 1 tablespoon dried thyme
- 1 tablespoon paprika
- 1 tablespoon brown sugar
- 1 tablespoon garlic powder
- 1 tablespoon onion powder
- 1 teaspoon cayenne pepper (adjust to taste for spiciness)
- 1 teaspoon ground cinnamon
- 1 teaspoon ground nutmeg
- 1 teaspoon kosher salt
- 1/2 teaspoon black pepper
- 2 cloves garlic, minced
- 2 tablespoons fresh lime juice
- 2 tablespoons olive oil

Instructions:

1. In a mixing bowl, combine the ground allspice, dried thyme, paprika, brown sugar, garlic powder, onion powder, cayenne pepper, ground cinnamon, ground nutmeg, kosher salt, black pepper, minced garlic, fresh lime juice, and olive oil.

2. Stir the ingredients together until they are well blended, creating a flavorful Caribbean Jerk Rub.

3. Taste the rub and adjust the level of spiciness or sweetness by adding more cayenne pepper or brown sugar to suit your preference.

4. Transfer the Caribbean Jerk Rub to an airtight container or a spice jar with a tight-fitting lid. Store it in a cool, dry place until ready to use.

Suggested Uses for Caribbean Jerk Rub:

1. Jerk Chicken: Rub chicken pieces or whole chickens with the Caribbean Jerk Rub before grilling or roasting. The combination of spices and citrus adds a flavorful and spicy kick.

2. Jerk Pork: Use the rub as a seasoning for pork chops, tenderloin, or ribs before grilling or slow-cooking for a taste of the

Caribbean.

3.   Jerk Shrimp Skewers: Coat shrimp with the rub before skewering and grilling for a spicy and aromatic seafood dish.

4.   Jerk Tofu or Tempeh: Marinate tofu or tempeh in the rub mixture before grilling or pan-frying. It adds a burst of Caribbean flavors to plant-based proteins.

5.   Jerk Marinade: Combine the rub with additional olive oil, lime juice, and a splash of soy sauce to create a marinade for various proteins. Allow the ingredients to meld for at least 30 minutes before cooking.

The Caribbean Jerk Rub is a bold and spicy seasoning blend that captures the vibrant flavors of Caribbean cuisine. It adds a tropical and spicy twist to a variety of dishes, making it a delightful addition to your culinary repertoire. Enjoy experimenting with different Caribbean-inspired recipes to showcase the deliciousness of this flavorful rub.

Sage and Lemon Rub Recipe

Ingredients:

- 2 tablespoons dried sage
- Zest of 2 lemons
- 2 tablespoons brown sugar
- 1 tablespoon dried thyme
- 1 tablespoon dried rosemary
- 1 teaspoon kosher salt
- 1/2 teaspoon black pepper
- 2 cloves garlic, minced
- 2 tablespoons olive oil

Instructions:

1.   In a mixing bowl, combine the dried sage, lemon zest, brown sugar, dried thyme, dried rosemary, kosher salt, black pepper, minced garlic, and olive oil.

2.   Stir the ingredients together until they are well blended, creating a flavorful Sage and Lemon Rub.

3.   Taste the rub and adjust the level of sweetness or herbal notes by adding more brown sugar or dried herbs to suit your preference.

4.   Transfer the Sage and Lemon Rub to an airtight container or a spice jar with a tight-fitting lid. Store it in a cool, dry place until ready to use.

Suggested Uses for Sage and Lemon Rub:

1.   Sage and Lemon Grilled Chicken: Rub chicken pieces or whole chickens with the Sage and Lemon Rub before grilling or roasting. The combination of sage and lemon creates a fragrant and savory flavor.

2.   Sage and Lemon Roasted Potatoes: Toss potato wedges or cubes in the rub before roasting for a flavorful and aromatic side dish.

3.   Sage and Lemon Roasted Vegetables: Coat a variety of vegetables like Brussels sprouts, carrots, and red onions in the Sage and Lemon Rub before roasting for a herbaceous and zesty side dish.

4.   Sage and Lemon Pasta: Sprinkle the rub over freshly cooked pasta and mix it with olive oil for a simple yet flavorful pasta dish. Add grated Parmesan cheese for extra richness.

5.   Sage and Lemon Marinade: Mix the rub with olive oil, lemon juice, and a touch of white wine vinegar to create a fragrant marinade for poultry or pork. Allow the ingredients to meld for at least 30 minutes before cooking.

The Sage and Lemon Rub is a versatile seasoning blend that combines the earthy notes of sage with the zesty brightness of lemon. It enhances the taste of a variety of dishes, making it a wonderful addition to your culinary repertoire. Enjoy experimenting with different recipes to showcase the deliciousness of this aromatic rub.

Honey Mustard and Dill Rub Recipe

Ingredients:

·   2 tablespoons yellow mustard seeds

·   2 tablespoons honey

·   2 tablespoons dried dill weed

·   1 tablespoon brown sugar

·   1 tablespoon dried parsley

·   1 teaspoon garlic powder

·   1 teaspoon onion powder

·   1 teaspoon kosher salt

·   1/2 teaspoon black pepper

·   Zest of 1 lemon

Instructions:

1.   In a mixing bowl, combine the yellow mustard seeds, honey, dried dill weed, brown sugar, dried parsley, garlic powder, onion powder, kosher salt, black pepper, and lemon zest.

2.   Stir the ingredients together until they are well blended, creating a flavorful Honey Mustard and Dill Rub.

3.	Taste the rub and adjust the level of sweetness or herbal notes by adding more honey or dried dill weed to suit your preference.

4.	Transfer the Honey Mustard and Dill Rub to an airtight container or a spice jar with a tight-fitting lid. Store it in a cool, dry place until ready to use.

Suggested Uses for Honey Mustard and Dill Rub:

1.	Honey Mustard and Dill Grilled Chicken: Rub chicken pieces or whole chickens with the Honey Mustard and Dill Rub before grilling or roasting. The blend of honey, mustard, and dill creates a flavorful and slightly sweet dish.

2.	Honey Mustard and Dill Salmon: Coat salmon fillets with the rub before grilling, baking, or pan-searing. It pairs perfectly with the rich flavors of salmon.

3.	Honey Mustard and Dill Roasted Potatoes: Toss potato wedges or cubes in the rub before roasting for a sweet and herbaceous side dish.

4.	Honey Mustard and Dill Salad Dressing: Mix the rub with olive oil, white wine vinegar, and a touch of honey for a delightful honey mustard and dill salad dressing.

5.	Honey Mustard and Dill Marinade: Combine the rub with additional honey, olive oil, and lemon juice to create a fragrant marinade for poultry, fish, or vegetables. Allow the ingredients to meld for at least 30 minutes before cooking.

The Honey Mustard and Dill Rub is a unique and flavorful seasoning blend that combines honey's sweetness, mustard's tanginess, and the dill's herbal notes. It enhances the taste of a variety of dishes, making it a delightful addition to your culinary repertoire. Enjoy experimenting with different recipes to showcase the deliciousness of this sweet and savory rub.

Southwest Chili Rub Recipe

Ingredients:

·	2 tablespoons chili powder

·	1 tablespoon ground cumin

·	1 tablespoon smoked paprika

·	1 tablespoon brown sugar

·	1 teaspoon garlic powder

·	1 teaspoon onion powder

·	1 teaspoon dried oregano

·	1 teaspoon kosher salt

·	1/2 teaspoon black pepper

·	1/2 teaspoon cayenne pepper (adjust to taste for spiciness)

- Zest of 1 lime

- 2 tablespoons olive oil

Instructions:

1.   In a mixing bowl, combine the chili powder, ground cumin, smoked paprika, brown sugar, garlic powder, onion powder, dried oregano, kosher salt, black pepper, cayenne pepper (adjust to taste), lime zest, and olive oil.

2.   Stir the ingredients together until they are well blended, creating a flavorful Southwest Chili Rub.

3.   Taste the rub and adjust the level of spiciness or sweetness by adding more cayenne pepper or brown sugar to suit your preference.

4.   Transfer the Southwest Chili Rub to an airtight container or a spice jar with a tight-fitting lid. Store it in a cool, dry place until ready to use.

Suggested Uses for Southwest Chili Rub:

1.   Southwest Chili Rubbed Steak: Rub steak cuts with the Southwest Chili Rub before grilling or pan-searing. The blend of spices and citrus adds a bold and zesty flavor.

2.   Southwest Chili Rubbed Chicken: Coat chicken pieces or whole chickens with the rub before grilling, roasting, or pan-frying for a spicy and aromatic dish.

3.   Southwest Chili Rubbed Shrimp: Season shrimp with the rub before skewering and grilling for a zesty and slightly spicy seafood dish.

4.   Southwest Chili Rubbed Vegetables: Toss a mix of bell peppers, red onions, and zucchini in the rub before grilling or roasting for a flavorful and colorful side dish.

5.   Southwest Chili Marinade: Mix the rub with additional olive oil and lime juice to create a tangy and spicy marinade for meats or vegetables. Allow the flavors to meld for at least 30 minutes before cooking.

The Southwest Chili Rub is a bold and spicy seasoning blend that captures the vibrant flavors of Southwestern cuisine. It adds a zesty and slightly spicy kick to a variety of dishes, making it a delightful addition to your culinary repertoire. Enjoy experimenting with different Southwestern-inspired recipes to showcase the deliciousness of this flavorful rub.

Smokey Paprika Rub Recipe

Ingredients:

- 2 tablespoons smoked paprika

- 1 tablespoon garlic powder

- 1 tablespoon ground cumin

- 1 teaspoon salt

- 1 teaspoon black pepper

- 1/2 teaspoon cayenne pepper (adjust to taste for spiciness)

Instructions:

1.	In a small mixing bowl, combine the smoked paprika, garlic powder, ground cumin, salt, black pepper, and cayenne pepper.

2.	Stir the ingredients together until they are thoroughly blended, creating a flavorful Smokey Paprika Rub.

3.	Taste the rub and adjust the level of spiciness by adding more or less cayenne pepper to suit your preference.

4.	Transfer the Smokey Paprika Rub to an airtight container or a spice jar with a tight-fitting lid. Store it in a cool, dry place until ready to use.

Suggested Uses for Smokey Paprika Rub:

1.	Grilled Meats: Rub the Smokey Paprika Rub generously onto steaks, chicken, pork chops, or ribs before grilling. It infuses a smoky and savory flavor into the meat.

2.	Smoked Brisket: Use the rub as a dry rub for smoked brisket. Apply it to the meat before smoking, allowing the flavors to meld during the slow cooking process.

3.	Grilled Vegetables: Sprinkle the Smokey Paprika Rub over vegetables like corn on the cob, bell peppers, or zucchini before grilling. It enhances the smoky notes of the grilled veggies.

4.	Smoked Salmon: Apply the rub to salmon fillets or whole salmon before smoking. It pairs perfectly with the smoky flavors of the fish.

5.	Tofu or Tempeh: Coat tofu or tempeh slices with the rub before grilling or pan-searing. It adds a smoky and slightly spicy kick to plant-based proteins.

The Smokey Paprika Rub is a versatile seasoning blend that pairs exceptionally well with dishes from a grilling and smoker cookbook. Its smoky, garlicky, and slightly spicy profile elevates the flavors of meats, vegetables, and even plant-based options. Enjoy experimenting with various grilled and smoked dishes to discover how this rub can enhance your culinary creations.

Greek Souvlaki Rub Recipe

Ingredients:

- 2 tablespoons dried oregano

- 1 tablespoon dried thyme

- 1 tablespoon dried rosemary

- 1 tablespoon dried parsley

- 1 tablespoon garlic powder

- 1 tablespoon onion powder

- 1 teaspoon paprika

- 1 teaspoon ground cumin

- 1 teaspoon ground coriander

- 1 teaspoon kosher salt

- 1/2 teaspoon black pepper

- Zest of 1 lemon

- 2 tablespoons olive oil

Instructions:

1.   In a mixing bowl, combine the dried oregano, dried thyme, dried rosemary, dried parsley, garlic powder, onion powder, paprika, ground cumin, ground coriander, kosher salt, black pepper, lemon zest, and olive oil.

2.   Stir the ingredients together until they are well blended, creating a flavorful Greek Souvlaki Rub.

3.   Taste the rub and adjust the level of spiciness or herbal notes by adding more black pepper or dried herbs to suit your preference.

4.   Transfer the Greek Souvlaki Rub to an airtight container or a spice jar with a tight-fitting lid. Store it in a cool, dry place until ready to use.

Suggested Uses for Greek Souvlaki Rub:

1.   Greek Souvlaki Skewers: Coat chicken, pork, or lamb cubes with the Greek Souvlaki Rub before skewering and grilling. Serve with pita bread and tzatziki sauce.

2.   Greek Souvlaki Marinade: Mix the rub with additional olive oil and lemon juice to create a zesty and herbaceous marinade for meats. Marinate for at least 30 minutes before grilling.

3.   Greek Souvlaki Roasted Potatoes: Toss potato wedges in the rub before roasting for a flavorful and aromatic side dish.

4.   Greek Souvlaki Salad Dressing: Combine the rub with olive oil, red wine vinegar, and a touch of Greek yogurt for a tangy and herb-infused salad dressing.

5.   Greek Souvlaki Rice: Mix the rub with cooked rice for a fragrant, flavorful Greek-inspired side dish.

The Greek Souvlaki Rub is a versatile seasoning blend that captures the essence of Greek cuisine with its aromatic herbs and zesty flavors. It enhances the taste of a variety of dishes, making it a wonderful addition to your culinary repertoire. Enjoy experimenting with different Greek-inspired recipes to showcase the deliciousness of this flavorful rub.

Maple Bourbon Glaze Recipe

Ingredients:

- · 1/2 cup maple syrup
- · 1/4 cup bourbon whiskey
- · 2 tablespoons brown sugar
- · 2 tablespoons Dijon mustard
- · 2 tablespoons apple cider vinegar
- · 1/2 teaspoon ground cinnamon
- · 1/4 teaspoon ground nutmeg
- · Pinch of kosher salt
- · Pinch of black pepper

Instructions:

1. In a saucepan over medium heat, combine the maple syrup, bourbon whiskey, brown sugar, Dijon mustard, apple cider vinegar, ground cinnamon, ground nutmeg, kosher salt, and black pepper.

2. Stir the ingredients together until they are well combined.

3. Bring the mixture to a simmer and reduce the heat to low. Allow it to simmer for about 5-7 minutes, or until the glaze thickens slightly.

4. Remove the saucepan from heat and let the Maple Bourbon Glaze cool for a few minutes. It will continue to thicken as it cools.

5. Transfer the glaze to a serving container or use it immediately to brush onto grilled ribs, chicken, salmon, or any other grilled meat or seafood.

Suggested Uses for Maple Bourbon Glaze:

1. Maple Bourbon Glazed Ribs: Brush the glaze onto grilled pork ribs during the last few minutes of cooking for sweet and smoky glazed ribs.

2. Maple Bourbon Glazed Chicken: Use the glaze to baste chicken pieces while grilling or roasting for a flavorful and sticky glaze.

3. Maple Bourbon Glazed Salmon: Brush the glaze onto salmon fillets before grilling or baking for a sweet and savory twist on salmon.

4. Maple Bourbon Glazed Vegetables: Toss grilled or roasted vegetables, such as sweet potatoes or Brussels sprouts, in the glaze for a delightful side dish.

5. Maple Bourbon Glazed Tofu: Brush the glaze onto tofu slices or cubes before grilling or pan-frying for a vegetarian option with a burst of flavor.

The Maple Bourbon Glaze is a sweet and smoky sauce that adds depth and richness to grilled meats, seafood, and vegetables. Its combination of maple syrup and bourbon whiskey creates a delightful flavor profile that pairs perfectly with a variety of dishes. Enjoy using this glaze to enhance the taste of your grilled creations.

Moroccan Ras el Hanout Rub Recipe

Ingredients:

- 2 tablespoons ground cumin
- 2 tablespoons ground coriander
- 2 tablespoons ground cinnamon
- 2 teaspoons ground ginger
- 2 teaspoons ground paprika
- 1 teaspoon ground turmeric
- 1 teaspoon ground cardamom
- 1 teaspoon ground cloves
- 1 teaspoon ground nutmeg
- 1/2 teaspoon ground black pepper
- 1/2 teaspoon cayenne pepper (adjust to taste for spiciness)
- 1/2 teaspoon kosher salt
- 1/4 teaspoon ground allspice

Instructions:

1. In a mixing bowl, combine the ground cumin, ground coriander, ground cinnamon, ground ginger, ground paprika, ground turmeric, ground car- damom, ground cloves, ground nutmeg, ground black pepper, cayenne pepper (adjust to taste), kosher salt, and ground allspice.

2. Stir the ingredients together until they are well blended, creating a flavorful Moroccan Ras el Hanout Rub.

3. Taste the rub and adjust the level of spiciness by adding more cayenne pepper if desired.

4. Transfer the Moroccan Ras el Hanout Rub to an airtight container or a spice jar with a tight-fitting lid. Store it in a cool, dry place until ready to use.

Suggested Uses for Moroccan Ras el Hanout Rub:

1. Moroccan Ras el Hanout Chicken: Rub chicken pieces with the Moroccan Ras el Hanout Rub before grilling, roasting, or sautéing for a fragrant and spiced dish.

2. Moroccan Ras el Hanout Lamb: Season lamb chops or leg of lamb with the rub before grilling or roasting for an aromatic and exotic flavor.

3. Moroccan Ras el Hanout Couscous: Sprinkle the rub over cooked couscous and toss with olive oil, dried fruits, and toasted nuts for a flavorful side dish.

4. Moroccan Ras el Hanout Roasted Vegetables: Toss a mix of root vegetables and bell peppers in the rub before roasting

for a fragrant and colorful side dish.

5.   Moroccan Ras el Hanout Hummus: Blend the rub with chickpeas, tahini, olive oil, and lemon juice to create a Moroccan--inspired hummus dip.

The Moroccan Ras el Hanout Rub is a versatile seasoning blend that captures the exotic and aromatic flavors of Moroccan cuisine. It adds a rich and complex flavor profile to a variety of dishes, making it a delightful addition to your culinary repertoire. Enjoy experimenting with different Moroccan-inspired recipes to showcase the deliciousness of this flavorful rub.

Garlic and Herb Rub Recipe

Ingredients:

- 2 tablespoons dried basil
- 2 tablespoons dried oregano
- 2 tablespoons dried thyme
- 2 tablespoons dried rosemary
- 2 tablespoons dried parsley
- 2 tablespoons garlic powder
- 1 tablespoon onion powder
- 1 teaspoon kosher salt
- 1/2 teaspoon black pepper
- 2 teaspoons red pepper flakes (adjust to taste for spiciness)

Instructions:

1.   In a mixing bowl, combine the dried basil, dried oregano, dried thyme, dried rosemary, dried parsley, garlic powder, onion powder, kosher salt, black pepper, and red pepper flakes (adjust to taste).

2.   Stir the ingredients together until they are well blended, creating a flavorful Garlic and Herb Rub.

3.   Taste the rub and adjust the level of spiciness by adding more or fewer red pepper flakes to suit your preference.

4.   Transfer the Garlic and Herb Rub to an airtight container or a spice jar with a tight-fitting lid. Store it in a cool, dry place until ready to use.

Suggested Uses for Garlic and Herb Rub:

1.   Garlic and Herb Grilled Chicken: Rub chicken pieces or whole chickens with the Garlic and Herb Rub before grilling or roasting. The combination of herbs and garlic creates a savory and aromatic flavor.

2.   Garlic and Herb Roasted Potatoes: Toss potato wedges or cubes in the rub before roasting for a flavorful and herba-

ceous side dish.

3.   Garlic and Herb Roasted Vegetables: Coat a mix of vegetables like bell peppers, zucchini, and cherry tomatoes in the rub before roasting for a fragrant and colorful side dish.

4.   Garlic and Herb Pasta: Sprinkle the rub over freshly cooked pasta and mix it with olive oil for a simple yet flavorful pasta dish. Add grated Parmesan cheese for extra richness.

5.   Garlic and Herb Marinade: Mix the rub with olive oil, white wine vinegar, and a touch of lemon juice to create a flavorful marinade for poultry, pork, or vegetables. Allow the ingredients to meld for at least 30 minutes before cooking.

The Garlic and Herb Rub is a classic and versatile seasoning blend that enhances the taste of a variety of dishes with its savory herbs and garlic. It's a wonderful addition to your culinary repertoire and can be used in a wide range of recipes. Enjoy experimenting with different dishes to showcase the deliciousness of this aromatic rub.

Indian Garam Masala Rub Recipe

Ingredients:

- 2 tablespoons ground cumin
- 2 tablespoons ground coriander
- 2 tablespoons ground cardamom
- 1 tablespoon ground cinnamon
- 1 tablespoon ground cloves
- 1 tablespoon ground nutmeg
- 1 tablespoon ground black pepper
- 1 tablespoon ground fennel seeds
- 1 teaspoon ground ginger
- 1 teaspoon ground turmeric
- 1/2 teaspoon cayenne pepper (adjust to taste for spiciness)
- 1/2 teaspoon kosher salt

Instructions:

1.   In a mixing bowl, combine the ground cumin, ground coriander, ground cardamom, ground cinnamon, ground cloves, ground nutmeg, ground black pepper, ground fennel seeds, ground ginger, ground turmeric, cayenne pepper (adjust to taste), and kosher salt.

2.   Stir the ingredients together until they are well blended, creating a flavorful Indian Garam Masala Rub.

3.   Taste the rub and adjust the level of spiciness by adding more or less cayenne pepper to suit your preference.

4.	Transfer the Indian Garam Masala Rub to an airtight container or a spice jar with a tight-fitting lid. Store it in a cool, dry place until ready to use.

Suggested Uses for Indian Garam Masala Rub:

1.	Indian Garam Masala Chicken: Rub chicken pieces with the Indian Garam Masala Rub before grilling, roasting, or sautéing for an aromatic and spiced dish.

2.	Indian Garam Masala Beef: Season beef cuts like sirloin or tenderloin with the rub before grilling or pan-searing for a flavorful and exotic flavor.

3.	Indian Garam Masala Vegetable Curry: Use the rub to season a vegetable curry with a blend of your favorite vegetables and coconut milk.

4.	Indian Garam Masala Rice: Mix the rub with cooked rice, toasted nuts, and dried fruits for a fragrant and flavorful side dish.

5.	Indian Garam Masala Marinade: Combine the rub with yogurt, lemon juice, and a touch of oil to create a spicy and aromatic marinade for meats or vegetables. Allow the flavors to meld for at least 30 minutes before cooking.

The Indian Garam Masala Rub is a complex and aromatic seasoning blend that captures the vibrant flavors of Indian cuisine. It adds a rich and exotic flavor profile to a variety of dishes, making it a delightful addition to your culinary repertoire. Enjoy experimenting with different Indian-inspired recipes to showcase the deliciousness of this flavorful rub.

Herb and Citrus Rub Recipe

Ingredients:

·	2 tablespoons dried basil

·	2 tablespoons dried oregano

·	2 tablespoons dried thyme

·	1 tablespoon dried rosemary

·	1 tablespoon dried parsley

·	Zest of 2 lemons

·	Zest of 2 oranges

·	2 tablespoons garlic powder

·	1 tablespoon onion powder

·	1 teaspoon kosher salt

·	1/2 teaspoon black pepper

·	1/2 teaspoon red pepper flakes (adjust to taste for spiciness)

Instructions:

1.   In a mixing bowl, combine the dried basil, dried oregano, dried thyme, dried rosemary, dried parsley, lemon zest, orange zest, garlic powder, onion powder, kosher salt, black pepper, and red pepper flakes (adjust to taste).

2.   Stir the ingredients together until they are well blended, creating a flavorful Herb and Citrus Rub.

3.   Taste the rub and adjust the level of spiciness by adding more or fewer red pepper flakes to suit your preference.

4.   Transfer the Herb and Citrus Rub to an airtight container or a spice jar with a tight-fitting lid. Store it in a cool, dry place until ready to use.

Suggested Uses for Herb and Citrus Rub:

1.   Herb and Citrus Grilled Chicken: Rub chicken pieces or whole chickens with the Herb and Citrus Rub before grilling or roasting. The combination of herbs and citrus creates a flavorful and aromatic dish.

2.   Herb and Citrus Roasted Potatoes: Toss potato wedges or cubes in the rub before roasting for a fragrant and zesty side dish.

3.   Herb and Citrus Roasted Vegetables: Coat a mix of vegetables like bell peppers, asparagus, and zucchini in the rub before roasting for a flavorful and colorful side dish.

4.   Herb and Citrus Pasta: Sprinkle the rub over freshly cooked pasta and mix it with olive oil for a simple yet flavorful pasta dish. Add grated Parmesan cheese for extra richness.

5.   Herb and Citrus Marinade: Combine the rub with olive oil, lemon juice, and a touch of Dijon mustard to create a zesty and herb-infused marinade for poultry, pork, or vegetables. Allow the ingredients to meld for at least 30 minutes before cooking.

The Herb and Citrus Rub is a bright and aromatic seasoning blend that combines the freshness of citrus with the savory notes of herbs. It enhances the taste of a variety of dishes, making it a delightful addition to your culinary repertoire. Enjoy experimenting with different recipes to showcase the deliciousness of this zesty rub.

Thai Red Curry Rub Recipe

Ingredients:

·   2 tablespoons red curry paste

·   2 tablespoons brown sugar

·   2 tablespoons fish sauce

·   2 tablespoons soy sauce

·   Zest of 1 lime

·   Juice of 1 lime

·   2 teaspoons ground coriander

- 2 teaspoons ground cumin

- 1 teaspoon ground turmeric

- 1/2 teaspoon cayenne pepper (adjust to taste for spiciness)

Instructions:

1.   In a mixing bowl, combine the red curry paste, brown sugar, fish sauce, soy sauce, lime zest, lime juice, ground coriander, ground cumin, and ground turmeric.

2.   Stir the ingredients together until they are well blended, creating a flavorful Thai Red Curry Rub.

3.   Taste the rub and adjust the level of spiciness by adding more or less cayenne pepper to suit your preference.

4.   Transfer the Thai Red Curry Rub to an airtight container or a spice jar with a tight-fitting lid. Store it in a cool, dry place until ready to use.

Suggested Uses for Thai Red Curry Rub:

1.   Thai Red Curry Chicken Skewers: Rub chicken pieces or chicken skewers with the Thai Red Curry Rub before grilling or broiling for a spicy and aromatic Thai-inspired dish.

2.   Thai Red Curry Shrimp: Season shrimp with the rub before sautéing or grilling for a zesty and flavorful seafood option.

3.   Thai Red Curry Vegetables: Toss a mix of vegetables like bell peppers, broccoli, and snap peas in the rub before stir--frying for a Thai-inspired vegetable dish.

4.   Thai Red Curry Rice: Mix the rub with cooked rice, coconut milk, and chopped fresh cilantro for a fragrant and flavorful side dish.

5.   Thai Red Curry Marinade: Combine the rub with coconut milk and a bit of peanut butter to create a creamy and spicy marinade for chicken, beef, or tofu. Allow the flavors to meld for at least 30 minutes before cooking.

The Thai Red Curry Rub is a bold and spicy seasoning blend that captures the vibrant flavors of Thai cuisine. It adds a rich and aromatic flavor profile to a variety of dishes, making it a delightful addition to your culinary repertoire. Enjoy experimenting with different Thai-inspired recipes to showcase the deliciousness of this flavorful rub.

Hickory Smoke and Brown Sugar Rub Recipe

Ingredients:

- 2 tablespoons brown sugar

- 2 tablespoons smoked paprika

- 1 tablespoon kosher salt

- 1 tablespoon black pepper

- 1 tablespoon garlic powder

- 1 tablespoon onion powder

- 1 tablespoon ground cumin

- 1 tablespoon ground coriander

- 1 teaspoon cayenne pepper (adjust to taste for spiciness)

Instructions:

1.   In a mixing bowl, combine the brown sugar, smoked paprika, kosher salt, black pepper, garlic powder, onion powder, ground cumin, ground coriander, and cayenne pepper (adjust to taste).

2.   Stir the ingredients together until they are well blended, creating a flavorful Hickory Smoke and Brown Sugar Rub.

3.   Taste the rub and adjust the level of spiciness by adding more or less cayenne pepper to suit your preference.

4.   Transfer the Hickory Smoke and Brown Sugar Rub to an airtight container or a spice jar with a tight-fitting lid. Store it in a cool, dry place until ready to use.

Suggested Uses for Hickory Smoke and Brown Sugar Rub:

1.   Hickory Smoke and Brown Sugar Ribs: Rub pork ribs with the Hickory Smoke and Brown Sugar Rub before smoking, grilling, or roasting for sweet and smoky ribs.

2.   Hickory Smoke and Brown Sugar Pulled Pork: Season a pork shoulder or pork butt with the rub before slow-cooking for tender and flavorful pulled pork.

3.   Hickory Smoke and Brown Sugar Chicken Wings: Coat chicken wings with the rub before baking or grilling for a sweet and smoky appetizer.

4.   Hickory Smoke and Brown Sugar Baked Beans: Add the rub to a pot of baked beans for a sweet and smoky twist on a classic side dish.

5.   Hickory Smoke and Brown Sugar Roasted Nuts: Toss mixed nuts in the rub before roasting for a flavorful and savory snack.

The Hickory Smoke and Brown Sugar Rub is a perfect combination of sweet and smoky flavors that enhances the taste of grilled meats, smoked dishes, and even side dishes like beans and nuts. It's a versatile rub that adds depth and richness to your cooking. Enjoy using it to create delicious and flavorful dishes.

Tandoori Spice Rub Recipe

Ingredients:

- 2 tablespoons ground cumin

- 2 tablespoons ground coriander

- 2 tablespoons ground paprika

- 2 tablespoons ground turmeric

- 1 tablespoon ground ginger

- 1 tablespoon ground cinnamon

- 1 tablespoon ground cardamom

- 1 tablespoon ground cloves

- 1 tablespoon ground nutmeg

- 1 teaspoon cayenne pepper (adjust to taste for spiciness)

- 1 teaspoon kosher salt

- 1/2 teaspoon black pepper

- 1/2 cup plain yogurt (for marinating)

Instructions:

1.   In a mixing bowl, combine the ground cumin, ground coriander, ground paprika, ground turmeric, ground ginger, ground cinnamon, ground cardamom, ground cloves, ground nutmeg, cayenne pepper (adjust to taste), kosher salt, and black pepper.

2.   Stir the dry ingredients together until they are well blended, creating a flavorful Tandoori Spice Rub.

3.   Taste the rub and adjust the level of spiciness by adding more or less cayenne pepper to suit your preference.

4.   To use the rub as a marinade, mix it with plain yogurt in a separate bowl. The yogurt will help tenderize the meat and provide a creamy base for the rub.

5.   Transfer the Tandoori Spice Rub to an airtight container or a spice jar with a tight-fitting lid. Store it in a cool, dry place until ready to use.

Suggested Uses for Tandoori Spice Rub:

1.   Tandoori Chicken: Marinate chicken pieces in the Tandoori Spice Rub and yogurt mixture for at least 2 hours, then grill, bake, or broil for a flavorful and aromatic Tandoori chicken dish.

2.   Tandoori Lamb: Season lamb chops or skewers with the rub and yogurt mixture before grilling or roasting for a fragrant and exotic flavor.

3.   Tandoori Paneer (Indian Cheese): Coat cubes of paneer cheese with the rub and yogurt mixture, then grill or pan-fry for a vegetarian Tandoori option.

4.   Tandoori Vegetables: Toss a mix of vegetables like bell peppers, onions, and mushrooms in the rub and yogurt mixture before grilling or roasting for a flavorful side dish.

5.   Tandoori Naan Bread: Sprinkle the rub on naan bread before grilling or baking for a savory and aromatic accompaniment to your Tandoori dishes.

The Tandoori Spice Rub is a fragrant and flavorful seasoning blend that captures the essence of Tandoori cuisine. Whether you're using it as a dry rub or a marinade, it adds an exotic and aromatic touch to a variety of dishes. Enjoy creating delicious Tandoori-inspired meals with this versatile rub.

Honey Sriracha Rub Recipe

Ingredients:

- 2 tablespoons honey
- 2 tablespoons Sriracha sauce
- 2 tablespoons brown sugar
- 1 tablespoon soy sauce
- 1 tablespoon garlic powder
- 1 tablespoon onion powder
- 1 teaspoon ground ginger
- 1/2 teaspoon kosher salt
- 1/2 teaspoon black pepper

Instructions:

1. In a mixing bowl, combine the honey, Sriracha sauce, brown sugar, soy sauce, garlic powder, onion powder, ground ginger, kosher salt, and black pepper.

2. Stir the ingredients together until they are well blended, creating a flavorful Honey Sriracha Rub.

3. Taste the rub and adjust the level of spiciness or sweetness by adding more Sriracha sauce or honey to suit your preference.

4. Transfer the Honey Sriracha Rub to an airtight container or a spice jar with a tight-fitting lid. Store it in a cool, dry place until ready to use.

Suggested Uses for Honey Sriracha Rub:

1. Honey Sriracha Grilled Chicken: Rub chicken pieces or chicken wings with the Honey Sriracha Rub before grilling for a sweet and spicy dish.

2. Honey Sriracha Glazed Salmon: Brush salmon fillets with the rub before grilling or baking for a sweet and zesty seafood option.

3. Honey Sriracha Shrimp Skewers: Season shrimp skewers with the rub before grilling for a flavorful and slightly spicy appetizer.

4. Honey Sriracha Tofu: Coat tofu slices or cubes with the rub before grilling or pan-frying for a vegetarian option with a burst of flavor.

5.   Honey Sriracha Stir-Fry: Use the rub as a sauce for stir-frying a mix of vegetables and protein for a quick and spicy stir-fry.

The Honey Sriracha Rub is a balance of sweet and spicy flavors that adds an exciting kick to grilled meats, seafood, and even stir-fries. Its versatility makes it a fantastic addition to your culinary repertoire, allowing you to create dishes with a touch of heat and sweetness. Enjoy experimenting with different recipes to showcase the deliciousness of this flavorful rub.

Mango Chili Lime Rub Recipe

Ingredients:

- 2 tablespoons dried mango powder (amchur)
- Zest of 2 limes
- Juice of 2 limes
- 2 tablespoons chili powder
- 2 tablespoons brown sugar
- 1 tablespoon kosher salt
- 1 teaspoon ground cumin
- 1/2 teaspoon ground coriander
- 1/2 teaspoon black pepper
- 1/4 teaspoon cayenne pepper (adjust to taste for spiciness)

Instructions:

1.   In a mixing bowl, combine the dried mango powder (amchur), lime zest, lime juice, chili powder, brown sugar, kosher salt, ground cumin, ground coriander, black pepper, and cayenne pepper (adjust to taste).

2.   Stir the ingredients together until they are well blended, creating a flavorful Mango Chili Lime Rub.

3.   Taste the rub and adjust the level of spiciness or sweetness by adding more cayenne pepper or brown sugar to suit your preference.

4.   Transfer the Mango Chili Lime Rub to an airtight container or a spice jar with a tight-fitting lid. Store it in a cool, dry place until ready to use.

Suggested Uses for Mango Chili Lime Rub:

1.   Mango Chili Lime Grilled Chicken: Rub chicken pieces or chicken thighs with the Mango Chili Lime Rub before grilling for a sweet, tangy, and slightly spicy dish.

2.   Mango Chili Lime Shrimp Skewers: Season shrimp skewers with the rub before grilling or broiling for a zesty and flavor-

ful seafood option.

3.   Mango Chili Lime Tofu Tacos: Coat tofu slices or cubes with the rub before grilling or pan-frying. Serve in tacos with your favorite toppings.

4.   Mango Chili Lime Corn on the Cob: Rub the mixture onto freshly grilled corn on the cob for a sweet and zesty side dish.

5.   Mango Chili Lime Dressing: Mix the rub with olive oil, a touch of honey, and lime juice to create a tangy and exotic salad dressing.

The Mango Chili Lime Rub combines the fruity sweetness of mango with the zesty kick of lime and a hint of spiciness. It's a versatile seasoning blend that adds a burst of flavor to a variety of dishes, making it a delightful addition to your culinary repertoire. Enjoy experimenting with different recipes to showcase the deliciousness of this flavorful rub.

Ranch Seasoning Rub Recipe

Ingredients:

- ·   2 tablespoons dried parsley
- ·   2 tablespoons dried dill weed
- ·   2 tablespoons dried chives
- ·   2 tablespoons garlic powder
- ·   2 tablespoons onion powder
- ·   1 tablespoon kosher salt
- ·   1 teaspoon black pepper
- ·   1 teaspoon dried thyme
- ·   1 teaspoon dried basil
- ·   1 teaspoon dried oregano

Instructions:

1.   In a mixing bowl, combine the dried parsley, dried dill weed, dried chives, garlic powder, onion powder, kosher salt, black pepper, dried thyme, dried basil, and dried oregano.

2.   Stir the ingredients together until they are well blended, creating a flavorful Ranch Seasoning Rub.

3.   Taste the rub and adjust the level of any seasoning to suit your preference.

4.   Transfer the Ranch Seasoning Rub to an airtight container or a spice jar with a tight-fitting lid. Store it in a cool, dry place until ready to use.

Suggested Uses for Ranch Seasoning Rub:

1.   Ranch Grilled Chicken: Rub chicken pieces with the Ranch Seasoning Rub before grilling or roasting for a savory and herby dish.

2.   Ranch Seasoned Roasted Potatoes: Toss potato wedges or cubes in the rub before roasting for a flavorful and herbed side dish.

3.   Ranch Seasoned Popcorn: Sprinkle the rub over freshly popped popcorn for a savory and addictive snack.

4.   Ranch Seasoned Salad: Mix the rub with Greek yogurt and a touch of buttermilk to create a creamy ranch dressing for salads or as a dip.

5.   Ranch Seasoned Roasted Vegetables: Coat a mix of vegetables like carrots, broccoli, and cauliflower in the rub before roasting for a flavorful side dish.

The Ranch Seasoning Rub captures the classic flavors of ranch dressing and can be used to add a savory and herby touch to a variety of dishes. Its versatility makes it a fantastic addition to your culinary repertoire, allowing you to infuse the taste of ranch into your cooking. Enjoy experimenting with different recipes to showcase the deliciousness of this flavorful rub.

Pesto Parmesan Rub Recipe

Ingredients:

- 2 tablespoons dried basil

- 2 tablespoons dried parsley

- 2 tablespoons grated Parmesan cheese

- 1 tablespoon pine nuts, toasted and finely chopped

- 1 tablespoon garlic powder

- 1 tablespoon onion powder

- 1 teaspoon kosher salt

- 1/2 teaspoon black pepper

- 1/4 teaspoon red pepper flakes (adjust to taste for spiciness)

Instructions:

1.   In a mixing bowl, combine the dried basil, dried parsley, grated Parmesan cheese, finely chopped toasted pine nuts, garlic powder, onion powder, kosher salt, black pepper, and red pepper flakes (adjust to taste).

2.   Stir the ingredients together until they are well blended, creating a flavorful Pesto Parmesan Rub.

3.   Taste the rub and adjust the level of spiciness by adding more or fewer red pepper flakes to suit your preference.

4.   Transfer the Pesto Parmesan Rub to an airtight container or a spice jar with a tight-fitting lid. Store it in a cool, dry place until ready to use.

Suggested Uses for Pesto Parmesan Rub:

1.   Pesto Parmesan Grilled Chicken: Rub chicken pieces with the Pesto Parmesan Rub before grilling or roasting for a savory and herby dish.

2.   Pesto Parmesan Pasta: Sprinkle the rub over freshly cooked pasta with a drizzle of olive oil for a simple yet flavorful pasta dish.

3.   Pesto Parmesan Roasted Vegetables: Toss a mix of vegetables like zucchini, cherry tomatoes, and bell peppers in the rub before roasting for a fragrant and herby side dish.

4.   Pesto Parmesan Pizza: Use the rub as a seasoning for pizza dough or sprinkle it on top of pizza with your favorite toppings for a delicious homemade pizza.

5.   Pesto Parmesan Popcorn: Sprinkle the rub over freshly popped popcorn for a savory and herby snack.

The Pesto Parmesan Rub combines the classic flavors of pesto and Parmesan cheese to add a burst of herby and cheesy goodness to a variety of dishes. Its versatility makes it a fantastic addition to your culinary repertoire, allowing you to create delicious meals with a hint of Italian-inspired flavor. Enjoy experimenting with different recipes to showcase the deliciousness of this flavorful rub.

Sesame Ginger Rub Recipe

Ingredients:

-       2 tablespoons toasted sesame seeds

-       2 tablespoons ground ginger

-       2 tablespoons brown sugar

-       1 tablespoon soy sauce

-       1 tablespoon garlic powder

-       1 tablespoon onion powder

-       1 teaspoon kosher salt

-       1/2 teaspoon black pepper

-       1/2 teaspoon red pepper flakes (adjust to taste for spiciness)

Instructions:

1.   In a mixing bowl, combine the toasted sesame seeds, ground ginger, brown sugar, soy sauce, garlic powder, onion powder, kosher salt, black pepper, and red pepper flakes (adjust to taste).

2.   Stir the ingredients together until they are well blended, creating a flavorful Sesame Ginger Rub.

3.   Taste the rub and adjust the level of spiciness or sweetness by adding more red pepper flakes or brown sugar to suit your preference.

4. Transfer the Sesame Ginger Rub to an airtight container or a spice jar with a tight-fitting lid. Store it in a cool, dry place until ready to use.

Suggested Uses for Sesame Ginger Rub:

1. Sesame Ginger Grilled Salmon: Rub salmon fillets with the Sesame Ginger Rub before grilling or baking for a flavorful and aromatic seafood dish.

2. Sesame Ginger Stir-Fry: Use the rub as a seasoning for stir-frying a mix of vegetables and protein for a quick and savory stir-fry.

3. Sesame Ginger Tofu Skewers: Coat tofu cubes with the rub before grilling or pan-frying for a vegetarian option with a burst of flavor.

4. Sesame Ginger Noodles: Toss cooked noodles in the rub with a splash of sesame oil for a flavorful and Asian-inspired noodle dish.

5. Sesame Ginger Vinaigrette: Mix the rub with rice vinegar, vegetable oil, and a touch of honey to create a zesty and sesame ginger vinaigrette for salads or as a marinade.

The Sesame Ginger Rub combines the nutty aroma of toasted sesame seeds with the zesty kick of ginger to create a versatile and flavorful seasoning blend. It adds an exotic and aromatic touch to a variety of dishes, making it a delightful addition to your culinary repertoire. Enjoy experimenting with different recipes to showcase the deliciousness of this flavorful rub.

Chimichurri Rub Recipe

Ingredients:

- 2 tablespoons dried parsley

- 2 tablespoons dried oregano

- 2 tablespoons dried thyme

- 2 tablespoons dried rosemary

- 2 tablespoons garlic powder

- 2 tablespoons red wine vinegar

- 1 tablespoon olive oil

- 1 tablespoon lemon juice

- 1 teaspoon kosher salt

- 1/2 teaspoon black pepper

- 1/2 teaspoon red pepper flakes (adjust to taste for spiciness)

Instructions:

1.   In a mixing bowl, combine the dried parsley, dried oregano, dried thyme, dried rosemary, garlic powder, red wine vinegar, olive oil, lemon juice, kosher salt, black pepper, and red pepper flakes (adjust to taste).

2.   Stir the ingredients together until they are well blended, creating a flavorful Chimichurri Rub.

3.   Taste the rub and adjust the level of spiciness by adding more or fewer red pepper flakes to suit your preference.

4.   Transfer the Chimichurri Rub to an airtight container or a spice jar with a tight-fitting lid. Store it in a cool, dry place until ready to use.

Suggested Uses for Chimichurri Rub:

1.   Chimichurri Grilled Steak: Rub steak with the Chimichurri Rub before grilling for a herby and tangy beef dish.

2.   Chimichurri Roasted Potatoes: Toss potato wedges or cubes in the rub before roasting for a flavorful and aromatic side dish.

3.   Chimichurri Grilled Vegetables: Coat a mix of vegetables like bell peppers, zucchini, and mushrooms in the rub before grilling for a herby and savory side dish.

4.   Chimichurri Marinade: Mix the rub with olive oil and red wine vinegar to create a classic chimichurri sauce for marinating meats or drizzling over grilled dishes.

5.   Chimichurri Pizza: Use the rub as a seasoning for pizza dough or sprinkle it on top of pizza with your favorite toppings for a delicious homemade pizza.

The Chimichurri Rub captures the bold and herby flavors of the classic Argentine condiment. It's a versatile seasoning blend that adds a burst of freshness and tanginess to grilled meats, vegetables, and more. Enjoy experimenting with different recipes to showcase the deliciousness of this flavorful rub.

Smoked Applewood Rub Recipe

Ingredients:

·   2 tablespoons smoked paprika

·   2 tablespoons brown sugar

·   1 tablespoon kosher salt

·   1 tablespoon black pepper

·   1 tablespoon garlic powder

·   1 tablespoon onion powder

·   1 tablespoon ground cumin

·   1 tablespoon ground coriander

- 1 teaspoon ground cinnamon

- 1/2 teaspoon cayenne pepper (adjust to taste for spiciness)

Instructions:

1.   In a mixing bowl, combine the smoked paprika, brown sugar, kosher salt, black pepper, garlic powder, onion powder, ground cumin, ground coriander, ground cinnamon, and cayenne pepper (adjust to taste).

2.   Stir the ingredients together until they are well blended, creating a flavorful Smoked Applewood Rub.

3.   Taste the rub and adjust the level of spiciness or sweetness by adding more cayenne pepper or brown sugar to suit your preference.

4.   Transfer the Smoked Applewood Rub to an airtight container or a spice jar with a tight-fitting lid. Store it in a cool, dry place until ready to use.

Suggested Uses for Smoked Applewood Rub:

1.   Smoked Applewood Grilled Pork: Rub pork chops or pork tenderloin with the Smoked Applewood Rub before grilling or smoking for a sweet and smoky pork dish.

2.   Smoked Applewood Roasted Vegetables: Toss a mix of vegetables like sweet potatoes, Brussels sprouts, and carrots in the rub before roasting for a flavorful and smoky side dish.

3.   Smoked Applewood BBQ Ribs: Coat ribs with the rub before slow- cooking or smoking for tender and smoky ribs.

4.   Smoked Applewood Chicken Wings: Season chicken wings with the rub before baking or grilling for a sweet and smoky appetizer.

5.   Smoked Applewood Baked Beans: Add the rub to a pot of baked beans for a sweet and smoky twist on a classic side dish.

The Smoked Applewood Rub combines the rich and smoky flavors of apple- wood with a hint of sweetness. It's a versatile seasoning blend that adds depth and richness to your cooking, particularly when grilling or smoking meats. Enjoy experimenting with different recipes to showcase the deliciousness of this flavorful rub.

Harissa Spice Rub Recipe

Ingredients:

- 2 tablespoons ground cumin

- 2 tablespoons ground coriander

- 2 tablespoons smoked paprika

- 2 tablespoons ground chili powder

- 2 tablespoons garlic powder

- 1 tablespoon ground caraway seeds
- 1 tablespoon ground cinnamon
- 1 teaspoon ground cayenne pepper (adjust to taste for spiciness)
- 1 teaspoon kosher salt
- 1/2 teaspoon black pepper

Instructions:

1.   In a mixing bowl, combine the ground cumin, ground coriander, smoked paprika, ground chili powder, garlic powder, ground caraway seeds, ground cinnamon, cayenne pepper (adjust to taste), kosher salt, and black pepper.

2.   Stir the ingredients together until they are well blended, creating a flavorful Harissa Spice Rub.

3.   Taste the rub and adjust the level of spiciness by adding more or less cayenne pepper to suit your preference.

4.   Transfer the Harissa Spice Rub to an airtight container or a spice jar with a tight-fitting lid. Store it in a cool, dry place until ready to use.

Suggested Uses for Harissa Spice Rub:

1.   Harissa-Spiced Grilled Chicken: Rub chicken pieces with the Harissa Spice Rub before grilling for a spicy and aromatic dish.

2.   Harissa-Spiced Roasted Vegetables: Toss a mix of vegetables like eggplant, bell peppers, and zucchini in the rub before roasting for a flavorful and spicy side dish.

3.   Harissa-Spiced Lamb Kebabs: Season lamb kebabs with the rub before grilling for a fragrant and spicy skewer dish.

4.   Harissa-Spiced Couscous: Mix the rub with cooked couscous, toasted nuts, and dried fruits for a flavorful and spicy side dish.

5.   Harissa-Spiced Hummus: Blend the rub into hummus for a spicy and exotic dip.

The Harissa Spice Rub captures the bold and fiery flavors of North African cuisine. It adds a spicy and aromatic touch to a variety of dishes, making it a delightful addition to your culinary repertoire. Enjoy experimenting with different recipes to showcase the deliciousness of this flavorful rub.

Lavender and Rosemary Rub Recipe

Ingredients:

- 2 tablespoons dried lavender flowers
- 2 tablespoons dried rosemary
- 1 tablespoon dried thyme

- 1 tablespoon dried oregano
- 1 tablespoon dried marjoram
- 1 tablespoon kosher salt
- 1 teaspoon black pepper
- 1 teaspoon garlic powder
- 1 teaspoon onion powder

Instructions:

1. In a mixing bowl, combine the dried lavender flowers, rosemary, thyme, oregano, marjoram, kosher salt, black pepper, garlic powder, and onion powder.

2. Stir the ingredients together until they are well blended, creating a flavorful Lavender and Rosemary Rub.

3. Taste the rub and adjust the level of any seasoning to suit your preference.

4. Transfer the Lavender and Rosemary Rub to an airtight container or a spice jar with a tight-fitting lid. Store it in a cool, dry place until ready to use.

Suggested Uses for Lavender and Rosemary Rub:

1. Lavender and Rosemary Grilled Lamb: Rub lamb chops or leg of lamb with the Lavender and Rosemary Rub before grilling or roasting for a fragrant and herbaceous dish.

2. Lavender and Rosemary Roasted Potatoes: Toss potato wedges or cubes in the rub before roasting for a flavorful and aromatic side dish.

3. Lavender and Rosemary Roasted Chicken: Season a whole chicken with the rub before roasting for a herby and delightful poultry dish.

4. Lavender and Rosemary Infused Olive Oil: Mix the rub with extra virgin olive oil and let it infuse for a few days. Use the infused oil for drizzling over salads or grilled vegetables.

5. Lavender and Rosemary Biscuits: Add a teaspoon of the rub to biscuit dough for a unique and savory biscuit variation.

The Lavender and Rosemary Rub combines the floral notes of lavender with the earthy aroma of rosemary to create a fragrant and herbaceous seasoning blend. It adds a delightful and aromatic touch to a variety of dishes, especially those featuring lamb or poultry. Enjoy experimenting with different recipes to showcase the deliciousness of this flavorful rub.

Pumpkin Spice Rub Recipe

Ingredients:

- 2 tablespoons ground cinnamon

- 1 tablespoon ground ginger

- 1 tablespoon ground nutmeg

- 1 tablespoon ground allspice

- 1 tablespoon ground cloves

- 1 tablespoon ground cardamom

- 1 tablespoon brown sugar

- 1 teaspoon kosher salt

Instructions:

1.   Combine the ground cinnamon, ginger, nutmeg, allspice, cloves, car- damom, brown sugar, and kosher salt in a mixing bowl.

2.   Stir the ingredients together until they are well blended, creating a flavorful Pumpkin Spice Rub.

3.   Taste the rub and adjust the level of sweetness or spice by adding more brown sugar or any other spice to suit your preference.

4.   Transfer the Pumpkin Spice Rub to an airtight container or a spice jar with a tight-fitting lid. Store it in a cool, dry place until ready to use.

Suggested Uses for Pumpkin Spice Rub:

1.   Pumpkin Spice Roasted Vegetables: Toss a mix of vegetables like sweet potatoes, butternut squash, and carrots in the rub before roasting for a sweet and aromatic side dish.

2.   Pumpkin Spice Coffee: Mix a pinch of the rub into your coffee grounds before brewing for a homemade pumpkin spice coffee.

3.   Pumpkin Spice Pancakes: Add a teaspoon of the rub to your pancake batter for a flavorful and seasonal breakfast.

4.   Pumpkin Spice Whipped Cream: Mix the rub with heavy cream and a touch of powdered sugar to create a spiced whipped cream for topping desserts.

5.   Pumpkin Spice Popcorn: Sprinkle the rub over freshly popped popcorn for a sweet and spiced snack.

The Pumpkin Spice Rub captures the warm and comforting flavors of fall with a blend of aromatic spices. It's a versatile seasoning blend that adds a cozy and seasonal touch to a variety of dishes, especially those with a hint of sweetness. Enjoy experimenting with different recipes to showcase the deliciousness of this flavorful rub, especially during the autumn season.

Gingerbread Spice Rub Recipe

Ingredients:

- 2 tablespoons ground cinnamon
- 1 tablespoon ground ginger
- 1 tablespoon ground allspice
- 1 tablespoon ground cloves
- 1 tablespoon ground nutmeg
- 1 tablespoon ground cardamom
- 2 tablespoons brown sugar
- 1 teaspoon kosher salt

Instructions:

1. In a mixing bowl, combine the ground cinnamon, ground ginger, ground allspice, ground cloves, ground nutmeg, ground cardamom, brown sugar, and kosher salt.

2. Stir the ingredients together until they are well blended, creating a flavorful Gingerbread Spice Rub.

3. Taste the rub and adjust the level of sweetness or spice by adding more brown sugar or any other spice to suit your preference.

4. Transfer the Gingerbread Spice Rub to an airtight container or a spice jar with a tight-fitting lid. Store it in a cool, dry place until ready to use.

Suggested Uses for Gingerbread Spice Rub:

1. Gingerbread Spice Cookies: Use the rub as a seasoning for gingerbread cookie dough for a spiced and flavorful batch of cookies.

2. Gingerbread Spice Latte: Mix a pinch of the rub into your latte or hot chocolate for a spiced and cozy beverage.

3. Gingerbread Spice Pancakes: Add a teaspoon of the rub to your pancake batter for a spiced and seasonal breakfast.

4. Gingerbread Spice Oatmeal: Sprinkle the rub over a bowl of oatmeal for a comforting and spiced morning meal.

5. Gingerbread Spice Whipped Cream: Mix the rub with heavy cream and a touch of powdered sugar to create a spiced whipped cream for topping desserts and beverages.

The Gingerbread Spice Rub captures gingerbread's warm and comforting flavors with a blend of aromatic spices. It's a versatile seasoning blend that adds a cozy and seasonal touch to a variety of sweet dishes and beverages, especially during the holiday season. Enjoy experimenting with different recipes to showcase the deliciousness of this flavorful rub.

Chai Spice Rub Recipe

Ingredients:

- 2 tablespoons ground cinnamon
- 1 tablespoon ground ginger
- 1 tablespoon ground cardamom
- 1 tablespoon ground cloves
- 1 tablespoon ground allspice
- 1 tablespoon ground nutmeg
- 1 tablespoon ground black pepper
- 1 teaspoon ground star anise (optional, for extra flavor)
- 2 tablespoons brown sugar
- 1 teaspoon kosher salt

Instructions:

1. In a mixing bowl, combine the ground cinnamon, ground ginger, ground cardamom, ground cloves, ground allspice, ground nutmeg, ground black pepper, ground star anise (if using), brown sugar, and kosher salt.

2. Stir the ingredients together until they are well blended, creating a flavorful Chai Spice Rub.

3. Taste the rub and adjust the level of sweetness or spice by adding more brown sugar or any other spice to suit your preference.

4. Transfer the Chai Spice Rub to an airtight container or a spice jar with a tight-fitting lid. Store it in a cool, dry place until ready to use.

Suggested Uses for Chai Spice Rub:

1. Chai Spice Latte: Mix a pinch of the rub into your latte, chai tea, or hot chocolate for a spiced and aromatic beverage.

2. Chai Spice Baked Goods: Use the rub as a seasoning for baked goods like muffins, cookies, and bread for a spiced and flavorful treat.

3. Chai Spice Oatmeal: Sprinkle the rub over a bowl of oatmeal for a comforting and spiced morning meal.

4. Chai Spice Whipped Cream: Mix the rub with heavy cream and a touch of powdered sugar to create a spiced whipped cream for topping desserts and beverages.

5. Chai Spice Roasted Nuts: Toss mixed nuts with melted butter and the rub before roasting for a flavorful and spiced snack.

The Chai Spice Rub captures chai tea's aromatic and exotic flavors with a blend of fragrant spices. It's a versatile seasoning blend that adds warmth and depth to a variety of dishes and beverages, making it a delightful addition to your culinary repertoire. Enjoy experimenting with different recipes to showcase the deliciousness of this flavorful rub.

Miso Sesame Rub Recipe

Ingredients:

- 2 tablespoons white miso paste

- 2 tablespoons toasted sesame seeds

- 1 tablespoon sesame oil

- 1 tablespoon brown sugar

- 1 tablespoon soy sauce

- 1 teaspoon garlic powder

- 1 teaspoon onion powder

- 1/2 teaspoon black pepper

Instructions:

1. In a mixing bowl, combine the white miso paste, toasted sesame seeds, sesame oil, brown sugar, soy sauce, garlic powder, onion powder, and black pepper.

2. Stir the ingredients together until they are well blended, creating a flavorful Miso Sesame Rub.

3. Taste the rub and adjust the level of sweetness or saltiness by adding more brown sugar or soy sauce to suit your preference.

4. Transfer the Miso Sesame Rub to an airtight container or a spice jar with a tight-fitting lid. Store it in the refrigerator until ready to use.

Suggested Uses for Miso Sesame Rub:

1. Miso Sesame Grilled Chicken: Rub chicken pieces with the Miso Sesame Rub before grilling for a savory and umami--rich dish.

2. Miso Sesame Glazed Salmon: Mix the rub with a touch of honey and use it as a glaze for baked or grilled salmon fillets.

3. Miso Sesame Tofu Stir-Fry: Coat tofu cubes with the rub before stir- frying with vegetables for a flavorful and vegetarian option.

4. Miso Sesame Roasted Brussels Sprouts: Toss Brussels sprouts in the rub before roasting for a nutty and savory side dish.

5. Miso Sesame Noodle Salad: Mix the rub with cooked noodles, fresh vegetables, and a sesame dressing for a flavorful and Asian-inspired salad.

The Miso Sesame Rub combines the rich and salty flavors of miso with the nutty aroma of sesame seeds to create a delicious umami seasoning blend. It adds depth and complexity to your dishes, especially when grilling or roasting meats and vegetables. Enjoy experimenting with different recipes to showcase the deliciousness of this flavorful rub.

4

Perfecting Marinades

What Is a Marinade?

A marinade is a flavorful liquid mixture used to soak and infuse ingredients with taste, tenderness, and moisture before cooking. Marinades are essential in the culinary world, enhancing the flavor and texture of proteins, vegetables, and even fruits. Understanding the fundamentals of marinades is crucial for elevating your culinary creations.

Characteristics of Marinades:

1.   Flavor Infusion: Marinades are designed to permeate ingredients, imparting flavor and complexity from the inside out.

2.   Tenderization: Marinades often contain acidic components that break down muscle fibers in proteins, resulting in more tender and succulent dishes.

3.   Moisture Retention: Marinades help ingredients retain moisture during cooking, preventing dryness and enhancing juiciness.

4.   Seasoning: In addition to flavor, marinades provide seasoning through the inclusion of herbs, spices, oils, and other ingredients.

5.   Customization: Marinades can be customized to suit various cuisines and dishes, making them versatile for different culinary adventures.

Types of Marinades

(Acidic, Oil-Based, and More)

There are several types of marinades, each with its own characteristics and applications. Understanding these types allows you to choose the right one for your specific cooking needs:

1.   Acidic Marinades: These marinades contain acidic components like vinegar, citrus juice, yogurt, or wine. The acidity tenderizes proteins, adds brightness, and complements rich flavors. Examples include lemon herb marinades for chicken and red wine marinades for beef.

2.   Oil-Based Marinades: Oil-based marinades feature oils like olive oil, sesame oil, or nut oils combined with flavor enhancers such as herbs, spices, and garlic. They coat ingredients for grilling, roasting, or sautéing, locking in moisture and flavor. Examples include rosemary and garlic- infused olive oil marinades for vegetables or seafood.

3.   Dry Marinades or Spice Rubs: These are essentially dry versions of marinades, consisting of spices, herbs, salt, and sometimes sugar. Dry marinades are applied directly to the surface of ingredients, forming a flavorful crust during cooking. Examples include spice rubs for ribs or seafood.

4.   Dairy-Based Marinades: Marinades incorporating dairy products like yogurt or buttermilk provide tenderness and cre-

aminess. They are commonly used in Indian and Middle Eastern cuisines for dishes like chicken tikka or shawarma.

5.   Alcohol-Based Marinades: Marinades that feature alcoholic beverages, such as wine, beer, or spirits, infuse ingredients with unique flavors. Beer-based marinades are popular for grilled meats, while wine-based marinades work well with poultry and seafood.

6.   Sweet Marinades: Sweet marinades often include honey, maple syrup, molasses, or brown sugar, adding sweetness and depth to dishes. They are excellent for creating caramelized exteriors when grilling or roasting.

Building Flavor Profiles:

Creating balanced and enticing flavor profiles is essential when crafting marinades. A well-constructed marinade typically consists of several key components:

1.   Acid: Provide acidity with ingredients like vinegar, citrus juice, yogurt, wine, or even buttermilk. Acid helps tenderize proteins and brightens the overall flavor.

2.   Oil: Include a base oil, such as olive oil or a nut oil, to provide moisture, carry flavors, and create a smooth consistency.

3.   Herbs and Spices: Season the marinade with a combination of fresh or dried herbs, spices, and seasonings that align with the cuisine or dish you're preparing.

4.   Aromatics: Enhance depth and complexity with aromatics like minced garlic, grated ginger, or finely chopped onions.

5.   Sweeteners: Balance acidity and enhance flavor with sweet elements like honey, brown sugar, or maple syrup.

6.   Salt: Season the marinade with salt to amplify the flavors and encourage moisture retention.

7.   Flavor Enhancers: Experiment with ingredients like soy sauce, Worces- tershire sauce, fish sauce, or hot sauce to introduce depth and umami.

Marinating Times and Methods:

Marinating involves soaking ingredients in the marinade to allow flavors to meld and penetrate. The marinating time and method can vary depending on the type of ingredient and the desired outcome:

1.   Marinating Times:

·   Proteins: Marinating times for proteins like meat, poultry, and fish typically range from 30 minutes to 24 hours. Delicate proteins like fish require shorter marinating times, while tougher cuts of meat can benefit from longer marination.

·   Vegetables: Vegetables, such as mushrooms, eggplant, or zucchini, can be marinated for 15 minutes to 2 hours, depending on their thickness and texture.

1.   Marinating Methods:

·   Refrigeration: Marinating ingredients in the refrigerator is crucial to prevent foodborne illnesses. Use a sealable container or a resealable plastic bag to keep the ingredients submerged in the marinade.

·   Turning and Massaging: Periodically turning or massaging the ingredi- ents while marinating ensures an even distribution of flavors.

·   Room Temperature: In some cases, marinating at room temperature for a short time (less than 2 hours) can be suitable for proteins like steaks or chicken breasts. However, always follow food safety guidelines.

·   Piercing or Scoring: For proteins, piercing or scoring the surface can help the marinade penetrate more effectively.

Understanding marinating times and methods allows you to tailor your approach to the specific ingredient and dish you're preparing. Perfecting the marinating process is essential for achieving exceptional flavor and tenderness in your culinary creations.

Marinade Recipes

Classic Italian Marinade Recipe

Ingredients:

- 1/4 cup extra-virgin olive oil
- 2 cloves garlic, minced
- 1/4 cup red wine vinegar
- 1 tablespoon Dijon mustard
- 1 teaspoon dried oregano
- 1 teaspoon dried basil
- 1 teaspoon dried thyme
- 1 teaspoon dried rosemary
- 1/2 teaspoon dried red pepper flakes (adjust to taste)
- 1 teaspoon kosher salt
- 1/2 teaspoon black pepper
- Zest and juice of 1 lemon

Instructions:

1. In a mixing bowl, combine the extra-virgin olive oil, minced garlic, red wine vinegar, Dijon mustard, dried oregano, dried basil, dried thyme, dried rosemary, dried red pepper flakes (adjust to taste), kosher salt, black pepper, and the zest and juice of 1 lemon.

2. Whisk the ingredients together until they are well combined, creating a flavorful Classic Italian Marinade.

3. Taste the marinade and adjust the level of spiciness or acidity by adding more red pepper flakes or lemon juice to suit your preference.

4. Transfer the Classic Italian Marinade to an airtight container or a glass jar with a tight-fitting lid. Store it in the refrigerator until ready to use.

Suggested Uses for Classic Italian Marinade:

1.   Classic Italian Grilled Chicken: Marinate chicken pieces in the Classic Italian Marinade before grilling for a flavorful and herby dish.

2.   Classic Italian Pasta Salad: Use the marinade as a dressing for a pasta salad with cooked pasta, cherry tomatoes, olives, and fresh basil.

3.   Classic Italian Vegetable Skewers: Coat a mix of vegetables like bell peppers, zucchini, and red onion in the marinade before grilling for a savory side dish.

4.   Classic Italian Marinated Steak: Marinate steak in the Classic Italian Marinade before grilling or pan-searing for a juicy and flavorful beef dish.

5.   Classic Italian Bruschetta: Drizzle the marinade over toasted bread slices and top with diced tomatoes, fresh basil, and mozzarella cheese for a classic Italian bruschetta.

The Classic Italian Marinade captures the essence of Italian cuisine with its combination of herbs, garlic, and bright lemon zest. It's a versatile marinade that adds depth and flavor to a variety of dishes, making it a delightful addition to your culinary repertoire. Enjoy experimenting with different recipes to showcase the deliciousness of this flavorful marinade.

Lemon Rosemary Marinade Recipe

Ingredients:

- ·   1/4 cup extra-virgin olive oil
- ·   Zest and juice of 1 lemon
- ·   2 cloves garlic, minced
- ·   1 tablespoon fresh rosemary leaves, finely chopped (or 1 teaspoon dried rosemary)
- ·   1 teaspoon dried thyme
- ·   1 teaspoon kosher salt
- ·   1/2 teaspoon black pepper

Instructions:

1.   In a mixing bowl, combine the extra-virgin olive oil, zest and juice of 1 lemon, minced garlic, fresh rosemary leaves (or dried rosemary), dried thyme, kosher salt, and black pepper.

2.   Whisk the ingredients together until they are well combined, creating a flavorful Lemon Rosemary Marinade.

3.   Taste the marinade and adjust the level of acidity or herbiness by adding more lemon juice or rosemary to suit your preference.

4.   Transfer the Lemon Rosemary Marinade to an airtight container or a glass jar with a tight-fitting lid. Store it in the refrigerator until ready to use.

Suggested Uses for Lemon Rosemary Marinade:

1.   Lemon Rosemary Grilled Chicken: Marinate chicken pieces in the Lemon Rosemary Marinade before grilling for a fresh and herby dish.

2.   Lemon Rosemary Roasted Potatoes: Toss potato wedges or cubes in the marinade before roasting for a flavorful and aromatic side dish.

3.   Lemon Rosemary Marinated Shrimp: Season shrimp with the marinade before grilling or sautéing for a zesty and delightful seafood dish.

4.   Lemon Rosemary Marinated Tofu: Coat tofu cubes with the marinade before grilling or pan-frying for a vegetarian option.

5.   Lemon Rosemary Vinaigrette: Use the marinade as a dressing for salads with mixed greens, cherry tomatoes, and feta cheese.

The Lemon Rosemary Marinade combines the bright and zesty flavors of lemon with the earthy aroma of rosemary. It's a versatile marinade that adds freshness and depth to your dishes, making it a delightful addition to your culinary repertoire. Enjoy experimenting with different recipes to showcase the deliciousness of this flavorful marinade.

Teriyaki Sauce Recipe

Ingredients:

- 1 cup soy sauce

- 1/2 cup water

- 1/2 cup brown sugar

- 1/4 cup honey

- 3 cloves garlic, minced

- 1 tablespoon fresh ginger, minced

- 2 tablespoons mirin (rice wine) or white wine (optional)

- 2 tablespoons cornstarch

- 1/4 cup cold water

Instructions:

1.   In a saucepan, combine the soy sauce, 1/2 cup water, brown sugar, honey, minced garlic, minced fresh ginger, and mirin (if using). Stir to combine.

2.   Place the saucepan over medium heat and bring the mixture to a simmer. Allow it to simmer for about 5-7 minutes, stirring occasionally, until the sugar is fully dissolved, and the sauce has slightly thickened.

3.   In a small bowl, mix the cornstarch and 1/4 cup cold water until the cornstarch is completely dissolved, creating a slurry.

4.   Slowly pour the cornstarch slurry into the simmering sauce, stirring constantly. Continue to cook for an additional 2-3 minutes, or until the sauce has thickened to your desired consistency.

5.   Remove the Teriyaki Sauce from heat and let it cool. It will continue to thicken as it cools.

6.   Taste the sauce and adjust the sweetness or saltiness by adding more brown sugar or soy sauce if needed.

7.   Transfer the Teriyaki Sauce to a jar or bottle with a tight-fitting lid. Store it in the refrigerator until ready to use.

Suggested Uses for Teriyaki Sauce:

1.   Teriyaki Chicken: Use the sauce to marinate chicken pieces before grilling, baking, or pan-searing for a sweet and savory chicken dish.

2.   Teriyaki Salmon: Brush the sauce onto salmon fillets before grilling or broiling for a flavorful seafood dish.

3.   Teriyaki Beef: Marinate beef cuts in the sauce before grilling or stir-frying for a delicious beef teriyaki.

4.   Teriyaki Stir-Fry: Add the sauce to a stir-fry with vegetables and your choice of protein for a quick and tasty meal.

5.   Teriyaki Glaze: Use the sauce as a glaze for vegetables, tofu, or skewers on the grill.

The Teriyaki Sauce combines the savory umami flavor of soy sauce with the sweetness of brown sugar and honey, along with the aromatic notes of garlic and ginger. It's a versatile sauce that adds a delightful sweet and salty taste to your dishes, making it a flavorful addition to your culinary repertoire. Enjoy experimenting with different recipes to showcase the deliciousness of this classic teriyaki sauce.

Chimichurri Sauce Recipe

Ingredients:

·   1 cup fresh parsley leaves, finely chopped

·   1/2 cup fresh cilantro leaves, finely chopped

·   4 cloves garlic, minced

·   1/4 cup red wine vinegar

·   1/2 cup extra-virgin olive oil

·   1 teaspoon dried oregano

·   1 teaspoon red pepper flakes (adjust to taste)

·   1/2 teaspoon kosher salt

·   1/4 teaspoon black pepper

Instructions:

1.   In a mixing bowl, combine the finely chopped fresh parsley leaves, finely chopped fresh cilantro leaves, minced garlic, red wine vinegar, extravirgin olive oil, dried oregano, red pepper flakes (adjust to your preferred level of spiciness), kosher salt, and black pepper.

2.   Stir the ingredients together until they are well combined, creating a flavorful Chimichurri Sauce.

3.   Taste the sauce and adjust the level of spiciness or acidity by adding more red pepper flakes or vinegar to suit your preference.

4.   Allow the Chimichurri Sauce to sit at room temperature for at least 30 minutes before serving to let the flavors meld together. You can also refrigerate it for later use.

Suggested Uses for Chimichurri Sauce:

1.   Chimichurri Marinated Steak: Drizzle the sauce over grilled or pan- seared steak for a fresh and herbaceous finish.

2.   Chimichurri Marinated Chicken: Marinate chicken pieces in the sauce before grilling or baking for a flavorful poultry dish.

3.   Chimichurri Grilled Shrimp: Brush the sauce onto shrimp before grilling or skewering for a zesty and aromatic seafood dish.

4.   Chimichurri Vegetables: Toss grilled or roasted vegetables in the sauce for a vibrant and herb-infused side dish.

5.   Chimichurri Dressing: Use the sauce as a dressing for salads with mixed greens, cherry tomatoes, and avocado.

Chimichurri Sauce is a vibrant and herbaceous sauce that originated in Argentina. It combines the freshness of herbs like parsley and cilantro with the zing of garlic and red pepper flakes. It's a versatile sauce that adds a burst of flavor and freshness to your dishes, making it a flavorful addition to your culinary repertoire. Enjoy experimenting with different recipes to showcase the deliciousness of this classic Chimichurri Sauce.

Honey Mustard Marinade Recipe

Ingredients:

- 1/4 cup Dijon mustard

- 1/4 cup honey

- 2 tablespoons extra-virgin olive oil

- 2 cloves garlic, minced

- 1 tablespoon white wine vinegar (or apple cider vinegar)

- 1 teaspoon dried thyme

- 1 teaspoon kosher salt

- 1/2 teaspoon black pepper

Instructions:

1.	In a mixing bowl, combine the Dijon mustard, honey, extra-virgin olive oil, minced garlic, white wine vinegar, dried thyme, kosher salt, and black pepper.

2.	Whisk the ingredients together until they are well combined, creating a flavorful Honey Mustard Marinade.

3.	Taste the marinade and adjust the level of sweetness or acidity by adding more honey or vinegar to suit your preference.

4.	Transfer the Honey Mustard Marinade to an airtight container or a glass jar with a tight-fitting lid. Store it in the refrigerator until ready to use.

Suggested Uses for Honey Mustard Marinade:

1.	Honey Mustard Grilled Chicken: Marinate chicken pieces in the Honey Mustard Marinade before grilling for a sweet and tangy dish.

2.	Honey Mustard Glazed Salmon: Use the marinade as a glaze for baked or grilled salmon fillets.

3.	Honey Mustard Marinated Pork Chops: Season pork chops with the marinade before grilling or pan-searing for a flavorful and tender pork dish.

4.	Honey Mustard Vegetable Skewers: Coat a mix of vegetables like bell peppers, mushrooms, and onions in the marinade before grilling for a sweet and tangy side dish.

5.	Honey Mustard Coleslaw Dressing: Use the marinade as a dressing for coleslaw with cabbage and carrots.

The Honey Mustard Marinade combines honey and mustard's sweet and tangy flavors. It's a versatile marinade that adds a delightful combination of sweetness and tanginess to your dishes, making it a flavorful addition to your culinary repertoire. Enjoy experimenting with different recipes to showcase the deliciousness of this flavorful marinade.

Tropical Pineapple Marinade Recipe

Ingredients:

- 1 cup pineapple juice

- 1/4 cup soy sauce

- 1/4 cup extra-virgin olive oil

- 2 cloves garlic, minced

- 2 tablespoons brown sugar

- 1 tablespoon lime juice

- 1 teaspoon ground ginger

- 1/2 teaspoon black pepper

- 1/2 teaspoon red pepper flakes (adjust to taste)

- 1/2 teaspoon kosher salt

Instructions:

1. In a mixing bowl, combine the pineapple juice, soy sauce, extra-virgin olive oil, minced garlic, brown sugar, lime juice, ground ginger, black pepper, red pepper flakes (adjust to taste), and kosher salt.

2. Whisk the ingredients together until they are well combined, creating a flavorful Tropical Pineapple Marinade.

3. Taste the marinade and adjust the level of sweetness or spiciness by adding more brown sugar or red pepper flakes to suit your preference.

4. Transfer the Tropical Pineapple Marinade to an airtight container or a glass jar with a tight-fitting lid. Store it in the refrigerator until ready to use.

Suggested Uses for Tropical Pineapple Marinade:

1. Tropical Pineapple Grilled Chicken: Marinate chicken pieces in the Tropical Pineapple Marinade before grilling for a sweet and tangy dish.

2. Tropical Pineapple Shrimp Skewers: Thread shrimp onto skewers and coat them in the marinade before grilling for a zesty and delightful seafood dish.

3. Tropical Pineapple Marinated Tofu: Coat tofu cubes with the marinade before grilling or pan-frying for a vegetarian option.

4. Tropical Pineapple Glazed Pork: Season pork chops or tenderloin with the marinade before grilling or roasting for a flavorful and juicy pork dish.

5. Tropical Pineapple Fruit Salad: Use the marinade as a dressing for a fruit salad with pineapple chunks, mango, and kiwi.

The Tropical Pineapple Marinade combines the tropical sweetness of pineapple with savory and zesty ingredients. It's a versatile marinade that adds a delightful combination of sweet, tangy, and spicy flavors to your dishes, making it a flavorful addition to your culinary repertoire. Enjoy experimenting with different recipes to showcase the deliciousness of this flavorful marinade.

Asian Sesame Marinade Recipe

Ingredients:

- 1/4 cup soy sauce

- 2 tablespoons toasted sesame oil

- 2 tablespoons rice vinegar

- 1 tablespoon honey

- 2 cloves garlic, minced

- 1 tablespoon fresh ginger, minced

- · 1 teaspoon red pepper flakes (adjust to taste)
- · 1/2 teaspoon black pepper
- · 1/2 teaspoon kosher salt
- · 2 green onions, thinly sliced (for garnish)

Instructions:

1. In a mixing bowl, combine the soy sauce, toasted sesame oil, rice vinegar, honey, minced garlic, minced fresh ginger, red pepper flakes (adjust to taste), black pepper, and kosher salt.

2. Whisk the ingredients together until they are well combined, creating a flavorful Asian Sesame Marinade.

3. Taste the marinade and adjust the level of sweetness or spiciness by adding more honey or red pepper flakes to suit your preference.

4. Transfer the Asian Sesame Marinade to an airtight container or a glass jar with a tight-fitting lid. Store it in the refrigerator until ready to use.

Suggested Uses for Asian Sesame Marinade:

1. Asian Sesame Grilled Chicken: Marinate chicken pieces in the Asian Sesame Marinade before grilling for a savory and aromatic dish.

2. Asian Sesame Stir-Fry: Use the marinade as a sauce for stir-frying a mix of vegetables, tofu, or your choice of protein.

3. Asian Sesame Marinated Salmon: Season salmon fillets with the mari- nade before baking or grilling for a sweet and savory seafood dish.

4. Asian Sesame Noodle Salad: Toss cooked noodles with the marinade, fresh vegetables, and sesame seeds for a flavor- ful and refreshing salad.

5. Asian Sesame Glazed Tofu: Coat tofu cubes with the marinade before baking or pan-frying for a vegetarian option.

The Asian Sesame Marinade combines the rich and savory flavors of soy sauce and sesame oil with a hint of sweetness and spice. It's a versatile marinade that adds depth and complexity to your dishes, making it a flavorful addition to your culinary repertoire. Enjoy experimenting with different recipes to showcase the deliciousness of this flavorful marinade. Garnish with thinly sliced green onions for an extra burst of freshness and color.

Mediterranean Greek Yogurt Marinade Recipe

Ingredients:

- · 1 cup Greek yogurt
- · 2 tablespoons extra-virgin olive oil
- · 2 cloves garlic, minced

- 1 tablespoon lemon juice
- 1 teaspoon dried oregano
- 1 teaspoon dried basil
- 1 teaspoon dried thyme
- 1 teaspoon dried rosemary
- 1 teaspoon kosher salt
- 1/2 teaspoon black pepper
- Zest of 1 lemon

Instructions:

1.   In a mixing bowl, combine the Greek yogurt, extra-virgin olive oil, minced garlic, lemon juice, dried oregano, dried basil, dried thyme, dried rosemary, kosher salt, black pepper, and the zest of 1 lemon.

2.   Stir the ingredients together until they are well combined, creating a flavorful Mediterranean Greek Yogurt Marinade.

3.   Taste the marinade and adjust the level of acidity or herbiness by adding more lemon juice or dried herbs to suit your preference.

4.   Transfer the Mediterranean Greek Yogurt Marinade to an airtight con- tainer or a glass jar with a tight-fitting lid. Store it in the refrigerator until ready to use.

Suggested Uses for Mediterranean Greek Yogurt Marinade:

1.   Mediterranean Greek Yogurt Marinated Chicken: Marinate chicken pieces in the Mediterranean Greek Yogurt Ma- rinade before grilling for a creamy and herby dish.

2.   Mediterranean Greek Yogurt Marinated Lamb: Season lamb chops with the marinade before grilling for a flavorful and tender meat dish.

3.   Mediterranean Greek Yogurt Marinated Vegetables: Coat a mix of vegetables like bell peppers, eggplant, and cher- ry tomatoes in the marinade before grilling for a creamy and savory side dish.

4.   Mediterranean Greek Yogurt Marinated Tofu: Coat tofu cubes with the marinade before grilling or pan-frying for a vegetarian option.

5.   Mediterranean Greek Yogurt Tzatziki Sauce: Use the marinade as a base for a creamy tzatziki sauce with grated cucumber, dill, and garlic.

The Mediterranean Greek Yogurt Marinade combines the creaminess of Greek yogurt with a blend of Mediterranean herbs and flavors. It adds richness and depth to your dishes, making it a flavorful addition to your culinary repertoire. Enjoy experimen- ting with different recipes to showcase the deliciousness of this flavorful marinade.

Cilantro Lime Marinade Recipe

Ingredients:

- 1/4 cup fresh lime juice (about 2-3 limes)
- Zest of 1 lime
- 1/4 cup extra-virgin olive oil
- 2 cloves garlic, minced
- 1/4 cup fresh cilantro leaves, chopped
- 1 teaspoon ground cumin
- 1 teaspoon ground coriander
- 1/2 teaspoon chili powder
- 1/2 teaspoon kosher salt
- 1/4 teaspoon black pepper

Instructions:

1. In a mixing bowl, combine the fresh lime juice, zest of 1 lime, extra-virgin olive oil, minced garlic, chopped fresh cilantro leaves, ground cumin, ground coriander, chili powder, kosher salt, and black pepper.

2. Whisk the ingredients together until they are well combined, creating a flavorful Cilantro Lime Marinade.

3. Taste the marinade and adjust the level of acidity or spiciness by adding more lime juice or chili powder to suit your preference.

4. Transfer the Cilantro Lime Marinade to an airtight container or a glass jar with a tight-fitting lid. Store it in the refrigerator until ready to use.

Suggested Uses for Cilantro Lime Marinade:

1. Cilantro Lime Grilled Chicken: Marinate chicken pieces in the Cilantro Lime Marinade before grilling for a zesty and herby dish.

2. Cilantro Lime Marinated Shrimp: Season shrimp with the marinade before grilling or sautéing for a zesty and delightful seafood dish.

3. Cilantro Lime Marinated Tofu: Coat tofu cubes with the marinade before grilling or pan-frying for a vegetarian option.

4. Cilantro Lime Marinated Vegetables: Toss vegetables like bell peppers, red onions, and zucchini in the marinade before grilling for a zesty and aromatic side dish.

5. Cilantro Lime Rice: Use the marinade as a drizzle over cooked rice or as a dressing for rice and bean salads.

The Cilantro Lime Marinade combines fresh lime and cilantro's bright and zesty flavors with a hint of spices. It's a versatile marinade that adds a refreshing and zesty kick to your dishes, making it a flavorful addition to your culinary repertoire. Enjoy experimenting with different recipes to showcase the deliciousness of this flavorful marinade.

Spicy BBQ Marinade Recipe

Ingredients:

- 1/2 cup ketchup
- 1/4 cup brown sugar
- 2 tablespoons apple cider vinegar
- 2 tablespoons Worcestershire sauce
- 2 cloves garlic, minced
- 1 tablespoon hot sauce (adjust to taste)
- 1 teaspoon smoked paprika
- 1/2 teaspoon chili powder (adjust to taste)
- 1/2 teaspoon cayenne pepper (adjust to taste)
- 1/2 teaspoon black pepper
- 1/2 teaspoon kosher salt

Instructions:

1. In a mixing bowl, combine the ketchup, brown sugar, apple cider vinegar, Worcestershire sauce, minced garlic, hot sauce (adjust to taste), smoked paprika, chili powder (adjust to taste), cayenne pepper (adjust to taste), black pepper, and kosher salt.

2. Stir the ingredients together until they are well combined, creating a flavorful Spicy BBQ Marinade.

3. Taste the marinade and adjust the level of spiciness or sweetness by adding more hot sauce or brown sugar to suit your preference.

4. Transfer the Spicy BBQ Marinade to an airtight container or a glass jar with a tight-fitting lid. Store it in the refrigerator until ready to use.

Suggested Uses for Spicy BBQ Marinade:

1. Spicy BBQ Grilled Chicken: Marinate chicken pieces in the Spicy BBQ Marinade before grilling for a fiery and smoky dish.

2. Spicy BBQ Pulled Pork: Season pork shoulder or butt with the marinade before slow-cooking for spicy pulled pork sandwiches.

3. Spicy BBQ Beef Ribs: Coat beef ribs with the marinade before slow- cooking or grilling for spicy and tender ribs.

4. Spicy BBQ Marinated Tofu: Coat tofu cubes with the marinade before grilling or pan-frying for a vegetarian option.

5. Spicy BBQ Baked Beans: Add the marinade to a pot of baked beans for spicy and smoky beans as a side dish.

The Spicy BBQ Marinade combines the bold flavors of ketchup, hot sauce, and spices for a fiery and smoky kick. It's a versatile marinade that adds heat and depth to your dishes, making it a flavorful addition to your culinary repertoire. Enjoy experimenting with different recipes to showcase the deliciousness of this flavorful marina

Citrus Chipotle Marinade Recipe

Ingredients:

- 1/4 cup orange juice
- Zest and juice of 1 lime
- 2 cloves garlic, minced
- 2 chipotle peppers in adobo sauce, minced (adjust to taste)
- 2 tablespoons honey
- 2 tablespoons extra-virgin olive oil
- 1 teaspoon ground cumin
- 1/2 teaspoon smoked paprika
- 1/2 teaspoon kosher salt
- 1/4 teaspoon black pepper

Instructions:

1. In a mixing bowl, combine the orange juice, zest and juice of 1 lime, minced garlic, minced chipotle peppers in adobo sauce (adjust to taste), honey, extra-virgin olive oil, ground cumin, smoked paprika, kosher salt, and black pepper.

2. Whisk the ingredients together until they are well combined, creating a flavorful Citrus Chipotle Marinade.

3. Taste the marinade and adjust the level of spiciness or sweetness by adding more chipotle peppers or honey to suit your preference.

4. Transfer the Citrus Chipotle Marinade to an airtight container or a glass jar with a tight-fitting lid. Store it in the refrigerator until ready to use.

Suggested Uses for Citrus Chipotle Marinade:

1. Citrus Chipotle Grilled Chicken: Marinate chicken pieces in the Citrus Chipotle Marinade before grilling for a smoky and zesty dish.

2. Citrus Chipotle Marinated Shrimp: Season shrimp with the marinade before grilling or sautéing for a spicy and delightful seafood dish.

3. Citrus Chipotle Marinated Tofu: Coat tofu cubes with the marinade before grilling or pan-frying for a vegetarian option.

4. Citrus Chipotle Marinated Steak: Marinate steak in the Citrus Chipotle Marinade before grilling or pan-searing for a flavorful and smoky beef dish.

5.   Citrus Chipotle Rice Bowl: Use the marinade as a drizzle over cooked rice or as a dressing for rice and vegetable bowls.

The Citrus Chipotle Marinade combines the bright and tangy flavors of citrus with chipotle peppers' smoky and spicy kick. It's a versatile marinade that adds depth and heat to your dishes, making it a flavorful addition to your culinary repertoire. Enjoy experimenting with different recipes to showcase the deliciousness of this flavorful

Maple Dijon Marinade Recipe

Ingredients:

- · 1/4 cup Dijon mustard
- · 1/4 cup pure maple syrup
- · 2 tablespoons apple cider vinegar
- · 2 cloves garlic, minced
- · 1 tablespoon extra-virgin olive oil
- · 1 teaspoon dried thyme
- · 1/2 teaspoon black pepper
- · 1/2 teaspoon kosher salt

Instructions:

1.   In a mixing bowl, combine the Dijon mustard, pure maple syrup, apple cider vinegar, minced garlic, extra-virgin olive oil, dried thyme, black pepper, and kosher salt.

2.   Whisk the ingredients together until they are well combined, creating a flavorful Maple Dijon Marinade.

3.   Taste the marinade and adjust the level of sweetness or acidity by adding more maple syrup or apple cider vinegar to suit your preference.

4.   Transfer the Maple Dijon Marinade to an airtight container or a glass jar with a tight-fitting lid. Store it in the refrigerator until ready to use.

Suggested Uses for Maple Dijon Marinade:

1.   Maple Dijon Glazed Salmon: Use the marinade as a glaze for baked or grilled salmon fillets.

2.   Maple Dijon Marinated Chicken: Marinate chicken pieces in the Maple Dijon Marinade before grilling for a sweet and savory dish.

3.   Maple Dijon Roasted Vegetables: Toss vegetables like carrots, Brussels sprouts, and sweet potatoes in the marinade before roasting for a flavorful and sweet side dish.

4.   Maple Dijon Marinated Pork Chops: Season pork chops with the marinade before grilling or pan-searing for a flavorful and tender meat dish.

5.   Maple Dijon Salad Dressing: Use the marinade as a dressing for salads with mixed greens, apples, and pecans.

The Maple Dijon Marinade combines the rich and savory flavors of Dijon mustard with the sweetness of pure maple syrup. It's a versatile marinade that adds a delightful combination of sweet and tangy flavors to your dishes, making it a flavorful addition to your culinary repertoire. Enjoy experimenting with different recipes to showcase the deliciousness of this flavorful marinade.

Lemongrass Coconut Marinade Recipe

Ingredients:

- 1/2 cup canned coconut milk

- 2 stalks lemongrass, outer layers removed, and finely chopped (or 2 tablespoons lemongrass paste)

- 2 cloves garlic, minced

- 1 tablespoon fresh ginger, minced

- Zest and juice of 1 lime

- 2 tablespoons soy sauce

- 2 tablespoons brown sugar

- 1 teaspoon ground coriander

- 1/2 teaspoon ground turmeric

- 1/2 teaspoon kosher salt

- 1/4 teaspoon black pepper

Instructions:

1.   In a mixing bowl, combine the canned coconut milk, finely chopped lemongrass (or lemongrass paste), minced garlic, minced fresh ginger, zest and juice of 1 lime, soy sauce, brown sugar, ground coriander, ground turmeric, kosher salt, and black pepper.

2.   Stir the ingredients together until they are well combined, creating a flavorful Lemongrass Coconut Marinade.

3.   Taste the marinade and adjust the level of sweetness or spiciness by adding more brown sugar or ground coriander to suit your preference.

4.   Transfer the Lemongrass Coconut Marinade to an airtight container or a glass jar with a tight-fitting lid. Store it in the refrigerator until ready to use.

Suggested Uses for Lemongrass Coconut Marinade:

1.   Lemongrass Coconut Grilled Shrimp: Marinate shrimp in the Lemon- grass Coconut Marinade before grilling or sautéing for a fragrant and tropical seafood dish.

2.   Lemongrass Coconut Marinated Chicken: Marinate chicken pieces in the Lemongrass Coconut Marinade before grilling or roasting for a creamy and aromatic dish.

3.   Lemongrass Coconut Marinated Tofu: Coat tofu cubes with the mari- nade before grilling or pan-frying for a vegetarian option.

4.   Lemongrass Coconut Rice: Use the marinade as a drizzle over cooked rice or as a dressing for rice and vegetable bowls.

5.   Lemongrass Coconut Noodle Soup: Use the marinade as a base for a flavorful lemongrass coconut noodle soup with vegetables and protein.

The Lemongrass Coconut Marinade combines the creamy richness of coconut milk with the aromatic and citrusy flavors of lemongrass. It's a versatile marinade that adds a tropical and fragrant twist to your dishes, making it a flavorful addition to your culinary repertoire. Enjoy experimenting with different recipes to showcase the deliciousness of this flavorful marinade.

Indian Tandoori Marinade Recipe

Ingredients:

- 1 cup plain yogurt
- 2 tablespoons lemon juice
- 2 cloves garlic, minced
- 1 tablespoon fresh ginger, minced
- 1 tablespoon ground coriander
- 1 tablespoon ground cumin
- 1 teaspoon ground turmeric
- 1 teaspoon paprika
- 1/2 teaspoon cayenne pepper (adjust to taste)
- 1/2 teaspoon kosher salt
- 1/4 teaspoon black pepper
- 1/4 teaspoon ground cinnamon
- 1/4 teaspoon ground cloves

Instructions:

1.	In a mixing bowl, combine the plain yogurt, lemon juice, minced garlic, minced fresh ginger, ground coriander, ground cumin, ground turmeric, paprika, cayenne pepper (adjust to taste), kosher salt, black pepper, ground cinnamon, and ground cloves.

2.	Stir the ingredients together until they are well combined, creating a flavorful Indian Tandoori Marinade.

3.	Taste the marinade and adjust the level of spiciness or acidity by adding more cayenne pepper or lemon juice to suit your preference.

4.	Transfer the Indian Tandoori Marinade to an airtight container or a glass jar with a tight-fitting lid. Store it in the refrigerator until ready to use.

Suggested Uses for Indian Tandoori Marinade:

1.	Tandoori Grilled Chicken: Marinate chicken pieces in the Indian Tan- doori Marinade before grilling for a fragrant and spiced dish.

2.	Tandoori Marinated Paneer: Coat cubes of paneer cheese with the marinade before grilling or pan-frying for a vegetarian option.

3.	Tandoori Marinated Vegetables: Toss a mix of vegetables like bell peppers, onions, and tomatoes in the marinade before grilling or roasting for a flavorful and colorful side dish.

4.	Tandoori Naan Pizza: Use the marinade as a base for making tandoori- flavored naan pizza with your favorite toppings.

5.	Tandoori Chicken Skewers: Thread marinated chicken onto skewers and grill them for a delicious appetizer or main course.

The Indian Tandoori Marinade combines a blend of aromatic spices with yogurt for a rich and flavorful base. It's a versatile marinade that adds complexity and warmth to your dishes, making it a flavorful addition to your culinary repertoire. Enjoy experimenting with different recipes to showcase the deliciousness of this flavorful marinade.

Pesto Marinade Recipe

Ingredients:

·	1 cup fresh basil leaves, packed

·	1/2 cup grated Parmesan cheese

·	1/2 cup pine nuts

·	2 cloves garlic, minced

·	1/2 cup extra-virgin olive oil

·	Zest and juice of 1 lemon

·	1/2 teaspoon kosher salt

·	1/4 teaspoon black pepper

Instructions:

1. In a food processor, combine the fresh basil leaves, grated Parmesan cheese, pine nuts, minced garlic, and pulse until finely chopped.

2. With the food processor running, slowly drizzle in the extra-virgin olive oil until the mixture is well blended and forms a thick paste.

3. Add the zest and juice of 1 lemon, kosher salt, and black pepper. Pulse a few times to incorporate these ingredients into the pesto.

4. Taste the pesto and adjust the level of acidity or saltiness by adding more lemon juice or salt to suit your preference.

5. Transfer the Pesto Marinade to an airtight container. Store it in the refrigerator until ready to use.

Suggested Uses for Pesto Marinade:

1. Pesto Marinated Grilled Chicken: Marinate chicken pieces in the Pesto Marinade before grilling for a flavorful and herby dish.

2. Pesto Marinated Shrimp: Season shrimp with the marinade before grilling or sautéing for a fragrant and delightful seafood dish.

3. Pesto Marinated Vegetables: Toss grilled or roasted vegetables like cherry tomatoes, asparagus, and bell peppers in the marinade for a vibrant and aromatic side dish.

4. Pesto Pasta Salad: Use the pesto as a dressing for pasta salad with fresh vegetables and mozzarella cheese.

5. Pesto Pizza: Spread the pesto on pizza dough as a delicious sauce, and top it with your favorite ingredients for a homemade pesto pizza.

The Pesto Marinade combines the fresh and herbaceous flavors of basil with the richness of Parmesan cheese and pine nuts. It's a versatile marinade that adds vibrancy and depth to your dishes, making it a flavorful addition to your culinary repertoire. Enjoy experimenting with different recipes to showcase the deliciousness of this flavorful marinade.

Sesame Ginger Marinade Recipe

Ingredients:

· 1/4 cup soy sauce

· 2 tablespoons rice vinegar

· 2 tablespoons sesame oil

· 1 tablespoon fresh ginger, minced

· 2 cloves garlic, minced

· 1 tablespoon honey

· 1 tablespoon toasted sesame seeds

- 1/2 teaspoon crushed red pepper flakes (adjust to taste)
- 1/4 teaspoon black pepper

Instructions:

1. In a mixing bowl, combine the soy sauce, rice vinegar, sesame oil, minced fresh ginger, minced garlic, honey, toasted sesame seeds, crushed red pepper flakes (adjust to taste), and black pepper.

2. Stir the ingredients together until they are well combined, creating a flavorful Sesame Ginger Marinade.

3. Taste the marinade and adjust the level of spiciness or sweetness by adding more crushed red pepper flakes or honey to suit your preference.

4. Transfer the Sesame Ginger Marinade to an airtight container or a glass jar with a tight-fitting lid. Store it in the refrigerator until ready to use.

Suggested Uses for Sesame Ginger Marinade:

1. Sesame Ginger Marinated Chicken: Marinate chicken pieces in the Sesame Ginger Marinade before grilling or stir-frying for a flavorful and aromatic dish.

2. Sesame Ginger Marinated Salmon: Season salmon fillets with the marinade before baking, grilling, or pan-searing for a delightful seafood dish.

3. Sesame Ginger Stir-Fry: Use the marinade as a sauce for stir-frying a mix of vegetables, protein, and cooked rice or noodles.

4. Sesame Ginger Marinated Tofu: Coat tofu cubes with the marinade before grilling or pan-frying for a vegetarian option.

5. Sesame Ginger Salad Dressing: Use the marinade as a dressing for salads with mixed greens, carrots, and cucumbers.

The Sesame Ginger Marinade combines the bold flavors of ginger and sesame with a touch of sweetness and heat. It's a versatile marinade that adds depth and complexity to your dishes, making it a flavorful addition to your culinary repertoire. Enjoy experimenting with different recipes to showcase the deliciousness of this flavorful marinade.

Pineapple Teriyaki Marinade Recipe

Ingredients:

- 1 cup pineapple juice
- 1/4 cup soy sauce
- 1/4 cup brown sugar
- 2 cloves garlic, minced
- 1 tablespoon fresh ginger, minced

- 2 tablespoons rice vinegar

- 1/2 teaspoon toasted sesame oil

- 1/4 teaspoon black pepper

Instructions:

1.   Combine the pineapple juice, soy sauce, brown sugar, minced garlic, fresh ginger, rice vinegar, toasted sesame oil, and black pepper in a mixing bowl.

2.   Stir the ingredients together until they are well combined, creating a flavorful Pineapple Teriyaki Marinade.

3.   Taste the marinade and adjust the level of sweetness or acidity by adding more brown sugar or rice vinegar to suit your preference.

4.   Transfer the Pineapple Teriyaki Marinade to an airtight container or a glass jar with a tight-fitting lid. Store it in the refrigerator until ready to use.

Suggested Uses for Pineapple Teriyaki Marinade:

1.   Pineapple Teriyaki Grilled Chicken: Marinate chicken pieces in the Pineapple Teriyaki Marinade before grilling for a sweet and savory dish.

2.   Pineapple Teriyaki Glazed Salmon: Use the marinade as a glaze for baked or grilled salmon fillets.

3.   Pineapple Teriyaki Marinated Shrimp: Season shrimp with the marinade before grilling, sautéing, or skewering for a delightful seafood dish.

4.   Pineapple Teriyaki Stir-Fry: Use the marinade as a sauce for stir-frying a mix of vegetables, protein, and cooked rice or noodles.

5.   Pineapple Teriyaki Marinated Tofu: Coat tofu cubes with the marinade before grilling, pan-frying, or stir-frying for a vegetarian option.

The Pineapple Teriyaki Marinade combines the sweetness of pineapple juice with the savory flavors of teriyaki sauce and aromatic ginger. It's a versatile marinade that adds a tropical twist to your dishes, making it a flavorful addition to your culinary repertoire. Enjoy experimenting with different recipes to showcase the deliciousness of this flavorful marinade.

Raspberry Balsamic Marinade Recipe

Ingredients:

- 1/2 cup fresh raspberries

- 1/4 cup balsamic vinegar

- 2 tablespoons olive oil

- 2 tablespoons honey
- 2 cloves garlic, minced
- 1/2 teaspoon dried basil
- 1/4 teaspoon black pepper
- 1/4 teaspoon kosher salt

Instructions:

1. Combine the fresh raspberries, balsamic vinegar, olive oil, honey, minced garlic, dried basil, black pepper, and kosher salt in a small saucepan.

2. Heat the mixture over low heat, stirring and mashing the raspberries with a fork as they soften. Continue to simmer for about 5-7 minutes, until the raspberries have broken down and the mixture has thickened slightly.

3. Remove the saucepan from heat and let the Raspberry Balsamic Marinade cool to room temperature.

4. Once cooled, strain the marinade through a fine-mesh sieve to remove raspberry seeds and any remaining solids. Transfer the liquid marinade to an airtight container or a glass jar with a tight-fitting lid.

5. Store the Raspberry Balsamic Marinade in the refrigerator until ready to use.

Suggested Uses for Raspberry Balsamic Marinade:

1. Raspberry Balsamic Marinated Chicken: Marinate chicken pieces in the Raspberry Balsamic Marinade before grilling or roasting for a sweet and tangy dish.

2. Raspberry Balsamic Glazed Salmon: Use the marinade as a glaze for baked or grilled salmon fillets.

3. Raspberry Balsamic Marinated Pork: Season pork chops or tenderloin with the marinade before grilling or pan-searing for a flavorful and fruity meat dish.

4. Raspberry Balsamic Salad Dressing: Use the marinade as a dressing for salads with mixed greens, goat cheese, and candied pecans.

5. Raspberry Balsamic Drizzle: Drizzle the marinade over roasted vegeta- bles, such as asparagus or Brussels sprouts, for a burst of fruity flavor.

The Raspberry Balsamic Marinade combines the sweet and tart notes of fresh raspberries with the rich depth of balsamic vinegar. It's a versatile marinade that adds a delightful fruity twist to your dishes, making it a flavorful addition to your culinary repertoire. Enjoy experimenting with different recipes to showcase the deliciousness of this flavorful marinade.

Thai Coconut Curry Marinade Recipe

Ingredients:

- 1 cup canned coconut milk
- 2 tablespoons Thai red curry paste
- 2 tablespoons soy sauce
- 2 tablespoons fresh lime juice
- 2 cloves garlic, minced
- 1 tablespoon fresh ginger, minced
- 1 tablespoon brown sugar
- 1/2 teaspoon ground turmeric
- 1/2 teaspoon kosher salt
- 1/4 teaspoon black pepper

Instructions:

1. In a mixing bowl, combine the canned coconut milk, Thai red curry paste, soy sauce, fresh lime juice, minced garlic, minced fresh ginger, brown sugar, ground turmeric, kosher salt, and black pepper.

2. Stir the ingredients together until they are well combined, creating a flavorful Thai Coconut Curry Marinade.

3. Taste the marinade and adjust the level of spiciness or sweetness by adding more Thai red curry paste or brown sugar to suit your preference.

4. Transfer the Thai Coconut Curry Marinade to an airtight container or a glass jar with a tight-fitting lid. Store it in the refrigerator until ready to use.

Suggested Uses for Thai Coconut Curry Marinade:

1. Thai Coconut Curry Marinated Chicken: Marinate chicken pieces in the Thai Coconut Curry Marinade before grilling, baking, or stir-frying for a rich and aromatic dish.

2. Thai Coconut Curry Marinated Shrimp: Season shrimp with the marinade before grilling, sautéing, or skewering for a flavorful and coconut-infused seafood dish.

3. Thai Coconut Curry Noodles: Use the marinade as a sauce for tossing with cooked noodles, vegetables, and protein for a Thai-inspired noodle dish.

4. Thai Coconut Curry Vegetables: Toss a mix of vegetables like bell peppers, zucchini, and broccoli in the marinade before grilling, roasting, or stir-frying for a creamy and flavorful side dish.

5. Thai Coconut Curry Soup: Use the marinade as a base for a creamy and aromatic Thai coconut curry soup with your choice of protein and vegetables.

The Thai Coconut Curry Marinade combines the creaminess of coconut milk with the bold and aromatic flavors of Thai red curry paste. It's a versatile marinade that adds depth and spice to your dishes, making it a flavorful addition to your culinary repertoire. Enjoy experimenting with different recipes to showcase the deliciousness of this flavorful marinade.

Blackened Cajun Marinade Recipe

Ingredients:

- 1/4 cup olive oil

- 2 tablespoons Cajun seasoning

- 1 tablespoon paprika

- 1 teaspoon dried thyme

- 1 teaspoon dried oregano

- 1 teaspoon garlic powder

- 1/2 teaspoon onion powder

- 1/2 teaspoon cayenne pepper (adjust to taste)

- 1/2 teaspoon kosher salt

- 1/4 teaspoon black pepper

- Zest and juice of 1 lemon

Instructions:

1. In a mixing bowl, combine the olive oil, Cajun seasoning, paprika, dried thyme, dried oregano, garlic powder, onion powder, cayenne pepper (adjust to taste), kosher salt, black pepper, and the zest and juice of 1 lemon.

2. Stir the ingredients together until they are well combined, creating a flavorful Blackened Cajun Marinade.

3. Taste the marinade and adjust the level of spiciness or acidity by adding more Cajun seasoning or lemon juice to suit your preference.

4. Transfer the Blackened Cajun Marinade to an airtight container or a glass jar with a tight-fitting lid. Store it in the refrigerator until ready to use.

Suggested Uses for Blackened Cajun Marinade:

1. Blackened Cajun Grilled Chicken: Marinate chicken pieces in the Black- ened Cajun Marinade before grilling or pan-searing for a spicy and flavorful dish.

2. Blackened Cajun Marinated Shrimp: Season shrimp with the marinade before grilling, sautéing, or skewering for a fiery and bold seafood dish.

3. Blackened Cajun Roasted Vegetables: Toss a mix of vegetables like bell peppers, okra, and corn in the marinade before roasting for a spicy and smoky side dish.

4. Blackened Cajun Tofu: Coat tofu cubes with the marinade before grilling or pan-frying for a vegetarian option.

5. Blackened Cajun Pasta: Use the marinade as a sauce for tossing with cooked pasta, vegetables, and your choice of protein for a spicy pasta dish.

The Blackened Cajun Marinade combines a blend of bold spices and smokiness with a touch of citrus from the lemon. It's a versatile marinade that adds heat and flavor to your dishes, making it a flavorful addition to your culinary repertoire. Enjoy experimenting with different recipes to showcase the deliciousness of this spicy marinade.

Honey Sriracha Marinade Recipe

Ingredients:

- 1/4 cup honey

- 2 tablespoons sriracha sauce (adjust to taste)

- 2 tablespoons soy sauce

- 2 cloves garlic, minced

- 1 tablespoon fresh ginger, minced

- 1 tablespoon rice vinegar

- 1 tablespoon sesame oil

- 1/4 teaspoon black pepper

Instructions:

1. In a mixing bowl, combine the honey, sriracha sauce (adjust to taste), soy sauce, minced garlic, minced fresh ginger, rice vinegar, sesame oil, and black pepper.

2. Stir the ingredients together until they are well combined, creating a flavorful Honey Sriracha Marinade.

3. Taste the marinade and adjust the level of spiciness or sweetness by adding more sriracha sauce or honey to suit your preference.

4. Transfer the Honey Sriracha Marinade to an airtight container or a glass jar with a tight-fitting lid. Store it in the refrigerator until ready to use.

Suggested Uses for Honey Sriracha Marinade:

1. Honey Sriracha Marinated Chicken Wings: Marinate chicken wings in the Honey Sriracha Marinade before baking, grilling, or frying for a sweet and spicy appetizer.

2. Honey Sriracha Glazed Salmon: Use the marinade as a glaze for baked or grilled salmon fillets.

3. Honey Sriracha Marinated Tofu: Coat tofu cubes with the marinade before grilling, pan-frying, or baking for a vegetarian option.

4. Honey Sriracha Stir-Fry: Use the marinade as a sauce for stir-frying a mix of vegetables, protein, and cooked rice or noodles.

5. Honey Sriracha Dipping Sauce: Serve the marinade as a dipping sauce for spring rolls, dumplings, or crispy tofu bites.

The Honey Sriracha Marinade combines the sweetness of honey with the bold spiciness of Sriracha sauce. It's a versatile marinade that perfectly balances sweetness and heat to your dishes, making it a flavorful addition to your culinary repertoire. Enjoy experimenting with different recipes to showcase the deliciousness of this flavorful marinade.

Garlic Parmesan Marinade Recipe

Ingredients:

- 1/4 cup olive oil
- 1/4 cup grated Parmesan cheese
- 4 cloves garlic, minced
- 1 tablespoon fresh parsley, finely chopped
- 1 teaspoon dried oregano
- 1/2 teaspoon dried basil
- 1/2 teaspoon kosher salt
- 1/4 teaspoon black pepper
- Zest and juice of 1 lemon

Instructions:

1. In a mixing bowl, combine the olive oil, grated Parmesan cheese, minced garlic, finely chopped fresh parsley, dried oregano, dried basil, kosher salt, black pepper, and the zest and juice of 1 lemon.

2. Stir the ingredients together until they are well combined, creating a flavorful Garlic Parmesan Marinade.

3. Taste the marinade and adjust the garlic, herbs, or acidity level by adding more minced garlic, fresh herbs, or lemon juice to suit your preference.

4. Transfer the Garlic Parmesan Marinade to an airtight container or a glass jar with a tight-fitting lid. Store it in the refrigerator until ready to use.

Suggested Uses for Garlic Parmesan Marinade:

1. Garlic Parmesan Marinated Chicken: Marinate chicken pieces in the Garlic Parmesan Marinade before grilling, baking, or pan-searing for a savory and cheesy dish.

2. Garlic Parmesan Marinated Shrimp: Season shrimp with the marinade before grilling, sautéing, or skewering for a flavorful seafood dish.

3. Garlic Parmesan Roasted Vegetables: Toss a mix of vegetables like broccoli, cauliflower, and carrots in the marinade before roasting for a cheesy and aromatic side dish.

4. Garlic Parmesan Pasta: Use the marinade as a sauce for tossing with cooked pasta and your choice of protein for a creamy and garlicky pasta dish.

5.   Garlic Parmesan Bread: Brush the marinade onto slices of bread before toasting for a delicious garlic Parmesan bread accompaniment.

The Garlic Parmesan Marinade combines the rich and savory flavors of garlic and Parmesan cheese with aromatic herbs and a hint of lemon zest. It's a versatile marinade that adds a burst of cheesy goodness to your dishes, making it a flavorful addition to your culinary repertoire. Enjoy experimenting with different recipes to showcase the deliciousness of this flavorful marinade.

Mango Habanero Marinade Recipe

Ingredients:

·   1 cup fresh mango, peeled and diced

·   1 habanero pepper, seeds removed and finely chopped (use gloves)

·   1/4 cup orange juice

·   2 tablespoons lime juice

·   2 cloves garlic, minced

·   2 tablespoons honey

·   1 tablespoon soy sauce

·   1/2 teaspoon ground cumin

·   1/2 teaspoon kosher salt

·   1/4 teaspoon black pepper

Instructions:

1.   In a blender or food processor, combine the fresh mango, finely chopped habanero pepper (use gloves when handling), orange juice, lime juice, minced garlic, honey, soy sauce, ground cumin, kosher salt, and black pepper.

2.   Blend the ingredients until you have a smooth and well-mixed Mango Habanero Marinade.

3.   Taste the marinade and adjust the level of spiciness or sweetness by adding more habanero pepper or honey to suit your preference.

4.   Transfer the Mango Habanero Marinade to an airtight container or a glass jar with a tight-fitting lid. Store it in the refrigerator until ready to use.

Suggested Uses for Mango Habanero Marinade:

1.   Mango Habanero Marinated Chicken: Marinate chicken pieces in the Mango Habanero Marinade before grilling or baking for a sweet and spicy dish.

2.   Mango Habanero Marinated Pork: Season pork chops or tenderloin with the marinade before grilling or roasting for a

flavorful and fiery meat dish.

3.	Mango Habanero Marinated Shrimp: Use the marinade as a seasoning for shrimp before grilling, sautéing, or skewering for a tropical and spicy seafood dish.

4.	Mango Habanero Salad Dressing: Use the marinade as a dressing for salads with mixed greens, avocado, and grilled chicken.

5.	Mango Habanero Dipping Sauce: Serve the marinade as a dipping sauce for spring rolls, chicken tenders, or grilled vegetables.

The Mango Habanero Marinade combines the sweet and tropical flavors of mango with the intense heat of habanero pepper. It's a versatile marinade that perfectly balances sweetness and spiciness to your dishes, making it a flavorful addition to your culinary repertoire. Enjoy experimenting with different recipes to showcase the deliciousness of this flavorful marinade.

Lavender Lemon Marinade Recipe

Ingredients:

·	Zest and juice of 2 lemons

·	2 tablespoons fresh lavender flowers, finely chopped

·	2 cloves garlic, minced

·	1/4 cup olive oil

·	1 tablespoon honey

·	1/2 teaspoon dried thyme

·	1/2 teaspoon kosher salt

·	1/4 teaspoon black pepper

Instructions:

1.	In a mixing bowl, combine the zest and juice of 2 lemons, finely chopped fresh lavender flowers, minced garlic, olive oil, honey, dried thyme, kosher salt, and black pepper.

2.	Stir the ingredients together until they are well combined, creating a flavorful Lavender Lemon Marinade.

3.	Taste the marinade and adjust the level of sweetness or acidity by adding more honey or lemon juice to suit your preference.

4.	Transfer the Lavender Lemon Marinade to an airtight container or a glass jar with a tight-fitting lid. Store it in the refrigerator until ready to use.

Suggested Uses for Lavender Lemon Marinade:

1.   Lavender Lemon Marinated Chicken: Marinate chicken pieces in the Lavender Lemon Marinade before grilling, baking, or pan-searing for a fragrant and citrusy dish.

2.   Lavender Lemon Marinated Salmon: Season salmon fillets with the marinade before grilling, roasting, or pan-searing for a delightful seafood dish.

3.   Lavender Lemon Marinated Tofu: Coat tofu cubes with the marinade before grilling, pan-frying, or baking for a vegetarian option.

4.   Lavender Lemon Salad Dressing: Use the marinade as a dressing for salads with mixed greens, goat cheese, and candied pecans.

5.   Lavender Lemon Drizzle: Drizzle the marinade over grilled vegetables like asparagus or zucchini for a burst of floral and citrusy flavor.

The Lavender Lemon Marinade combines the bright and zesty notes of lemon with the delicate aroma of fresh lavender. It's a unique and aromatic marinade that adds a touch of elegance to your dishes, making it a flavorful addition to your culinary repertoire. Enjoy experimenting with different recipes to showcase the delightful flavor of this unique marinade.

Smoky Chipotle Lime Marinade Recipe

Ingredients:

·   Zest and juice of 2 limes

·   2 chipotle peppers in adobo sauce, minced

·   1/4 cup olive oil

·   2 cloves garlic, minced

·   1 tablespoon honey

·   1 teaspoon smoked paprika

·   1/2 teaspoon ground cumin

·   1/2 teaspoon kosher salt

·   1/4 teaspoon black pepper

Instructions:

1.   In a mixing bowl, combine the zest and juice of 2 limes, minced chipotle peppers in adobo sauce, olive oil, minced garlic, honey, smoked paprika, ground cumin, kosher salt, and black pepper.

2.   Stir the ingredients together until they are well combined, creating a flavorful Smoky Chipotle Lime Marinade.

3.   Taste the marinade and adjust the level of spiciness or sweetness by adding more minced chipotle peppers or honey to suit your preference.

4.   Transfer the Smoky Chipotle Lime Marinade to an airtight container or a glass jar with a tight-fitting lid. Store it in the

refrigerator until ready to use.

Suggested Uses for Smoky Chipotle Lime Marinade:

1.   Smoky Chipotle Lime Marinated Chicken: Marinate chicken pieces in the Smoky Chipotle Lime Marinade before grilling, baking, or pan-searing for a smoky and spicy dish.

2.   Smoky Chipotle Lime Marinated Shrimp: Season shrimp with the marinade before grilling, sautéing, or skewering for a fiery and citrusy seafood dish.

3.   Smoky Chipotle Lime Marinated Pork: Season pork chops or tenderloin with the marinade before grilling or roasting for a flavorful and smoky meat dish.

4.   Smoky Chipotle Lime Grilled Vegetables: Toss a mix of vegetables like bell peppers, onions, and zucchini in the marinade before grilling for a smoky and zesty side dish.

5.   Smoky Chipotle Lime Tofu Tacos: Use the marinade as a sauce for marinating and grilling tofu for delicious vegetarian tacos.

The Smoky Chipotle Lime Marinade combines chipotle peppers' smokiness with lime's zesty freshness. It's a flavorful and slightly spicy marinade that adds depth and citrusy notes to your dishes, making it a delightful addition to your culinary repertoire. Enjoy experimenting with different recipes to showcase this marinade's smoky and citrusy flavor.

Ginger Soy Marinade Recipe

Ingredients:
- 1/4 cup soy sauce
- 2 tablespoons rice vinegar
- 2 tablespoons sesame oil
- 1 tablespoon fresh ginger, minced
- 2 cloves garlic, minced
- 1 tablespoon honey
- 1/2 teaspoon crushed red pepper flakes (adjust to taste)
- 1/2 teaspoon kosher salt
- 1/4 teaspoon black pepper

Instructions:

1.   In a mixing bowl, combine the soy sauce, rice vinegar, sesame oil, minced fresh ginger, minced garlic, honey, crushed

red pepper flakes (adjust to taste), kosher salt, and black pepper.

2.　　Stir the ingredients together until they are well combined, creating a flavorful Ginger Soy Marinade.

3.　　Taste the marinade and adjust the level of spiciness or sweetness by adding more crushed red pepper flakes or honey to suit your preference.

4.　　Transfer the Ginger Soy Marinade to an airtight container or a glass jar with a tight-fitting lid. Store it in the refrigerator until ready to use.

Suggested Uses for Ginger Soy Marinade:

1.　　Ginger Soy Marinated Chicken: Marinate chicken pieces in the Ginger Soy Marinade before grilling, baking, or stir-frying for a savory and aromatic dish.

2.　　Ginger Soy Marinated Salmon: Season salmon fillets with the marinade before grilling, roasting, or pan-searing for a flavorful seafood dish.

3.　　Ginger Soy Marinated Tofu: Coat tofu cubes with the marinade before grilling, pan-frying, or stir-frying for a vegetarian option.

4.　　Ginger Soy Stir-Fry: Use the marinade as a sauce for stir-frying a mix of vegetables, protein, and cooked rice or noodles.

5.　　Ginger Soy Salad Dressing: Use the marinade as a dressing for salads with mixed greens, grilled chicken, and sliced almonds.

The Ginger Soy Marinade combines the umami richness of soy sauce with the fresh and spicy kick of ginger. It's a versatile marinade that adds depth and a hint of heat to your dishes, making it a flavorful addition to your culinary repertoire. Enjoy experimenting with different recipes to showcase the deliciousness of this aromatic marinade.

Pineapple Ginger Marinade Recipe

Ingredients:

- 1 cup pineapple juice

- 2 tablespoons soy sauce

- 2 tablespoons fresh ginger, minced

- 2 cloves garlic, minced

- 2 tablespoons brown sugar

- 1 tablespoon rice vinegar

- 1/2 teaspoon crushed red pepper flakes (adjust to taste)

- 1/2 teaspoon kosher salt

- 1/4 teaspoon black pepper

Instructions:

1. In a mixing bowl, combine the pineapple juice, soy sauce, minced fresh ginger, minced garlic, brown sugar, rice vinegar, crushed red pepper flakes (adjust to taste), kosher salt, and black pepper.

2. Stir the ingredients together until they are well combined, creating a flavorful Pineapple Ginger Marinade.

3. Taste the marinade and adjust the level of spiciness or sweetness by adding more crushed red pepper flakes or brown sugar to suit your preference.

4. Transfer the Pineapple Ginger Marinade to an airtight container or a glass jar with a tight-fitting lid. Store it in the refrigerator until ready to use.

Suggested Uses for Pineapple Ginger Marinade:

1. Pineapple Ginger Marinated Chicken: Marinate chicken pieces in the Pineapple Ginger Marinade before grilling, baking, or pan-searing for a tropical and savory dish.

2. Pineapple Ginger Marinated Shrimp: Season shrimp with the marinade before grilling, sautéing, or skewering for a sweet and zesty seafood dish.

3. Pineapple Ginger Marinated Pork: Season pork chops or tenderloin with the marinade before grilling or roasting for a flavorful and tropical meat dish.

4. Pineapple Ginger Stir-Fry: Use the marinade as a sauce for stir-frying a mix of vegetables, protein, and cooked rice or noodles.

5. Pineapple Ginger Glazed Salmon: Use the marinade as a glaze for baked or grilled salmon fillets.

The Pineapple Ginger Marinade combines the sweetness of pineapple juice with the aromatic and spicy notes of fresh ginger. It's a versatile marinade that adds a delightful tropical twist to your dishes, making it a flavorful addition to your culinary repertoire. Enjoy experimenting with different recipes to showcase the deliciousness of this sweet and zesty marinade.

Raspberry Chipotle Marinade Recipe

Ingredients:

- 1/2 cup fresh raspberries
- 2 chipotle peppers in adobo sauce, minced
- 2 cloves garlic, minced
- 1/4 cup balsamic vinegar
- 2 tablespoons olive oil
- 2 tablespoons honey

- 1/2 teaspoon kosher salt

- 1/4 teaspoon black pepper

Instructions:

1.   In a mixing bowl, combine the fresh raspberries, minced chipotle peppers in adobo sauce, minced garlic, balsamic vinegar, olive oil, honey, kosher salt, and black pepper.

2.   Use a fork to mash and stir the raspberries, incorporating them into the mixture, creating a flavorful Raspberry Chipotle Marinade.

3.   Taste the marinade and adjust the level of spiciness or sweetness by adding more minced chipotle peppers or honey to suit your preference.

4.   Transfer the Raspberry Chipotle Marinade to an airtight container or a glass jar with a tight-fitting lid. Store it in the refrigerator until ready to use.

Suggested Uses for Raspberry Chipotle Marinade:

1.   Raspberry Chipotle Marinated Chicken: Marinate chicken pieces in the Raspberry Chipotle Marinade before grilling, baking, or pan-searing for a sweet and spicy dish.

2.   Raspberry Chipotle Marinated Pork: Season pork chops or tenderloin with the marinade before grilling or roasting for a flavorful, fruity meat dish.

3.   Raspberry Chipotle Glazed Salmon: Use the marinade as a glaze for baked or grilled salmon fillets.

4.   Raspberry Chipotle Salad Dressing: Use the marinade as a dressing for salads with mixed greens, goat cheese, and candied pecans.

5.   Raspberry Chipotle Dipping Sauce: Serve the marinade as a dipping sauce for chicken tenders, spring rolls, or grilled vegetables.

The Raspberry Chipotle Marinade combines the sweetness of fresh raspberries with the smoky heat of chipotle peppers. It's a versatile marinade that adds a unique and bold flavor profile to your dishes, making it a flavorful addition to your culinary repertoire. Enjoy experimenting with different recipes to showcase the deliciousness of this sweet and spicy marinade.

Rosemary Balsamic Marinade Recipe

Ingredients:

- 1/4 cup balsamic vinegar

- 2 tablespoons olive oil

- 2 cloves garlic, minced

- 1 tablespoon fresh rosemary leaves, finely chopped

- 1 tablespoon honey
- 1/2 teaspoon kosher salt
- 1/4 teaspoon black pepper

Instructions:

1.   Combine the balsamic vinegar, olive oil, minced garlic, finely chopped fresh rosemary leaves, honey, kosher salt, and black pepper in a mixing bowl.

2.   Stir the ingredients together until they are well combined, creating a flavorful Rosemary Balsamic Marinade.

3.   Taste the marinade and adjust the level of sweetness or herbiness by adding more honey or fresh rosemary to suit your preference.

4.   Transfer the Rosemary Balsamic Marinade to an airtight container or a glass jar with a tight-fitting lid. Store it in the refrigerator until ready to use.

Suggested Uses for Rosemary Balsamic Marinade:

1.   Rosemary Balsamic Marinated Chicken: Marinate chicken pieces in the Rosemary Balsamic Marinade before grilling, baking, or pan-searing for a savory and aromatic dish.

2.   Rosemary Balsamic Marinated Beef: Season beef steaks or roasts with the marinade before grilling or roasting for a flavorful and herb-infused meat dish.

3.   Rosemary Balsamic Roasted Vegetables: Toss a mix of vegetables like potatoes, carrots, and Brussels sprouts in the marinade before roasting for a savory and herbaceous side dish.

4.   Rosemary Balsamic Marinated Portobello Mushrooms: Use the mari- nade to marinate and grill Portobello mushroom caps for a delicious vegetarian option.

5.   Rosemary Balsamic Salad Dressing: Use the marinade as a dressing for salads with mixed greens, cherry tomatoes, and feta cheese.

The Rosemary Balsamic Marinade combines balsamic vinegar's bold and tangy flavors with the aromatic notes of fresh rosemary. It's a versatile marinade that adds a delightful herbaceous touch to your dishes, making it a flavorful addition to your culinary repertoire. Enjoy experimenting with different recipes to showcase the deliciousness of this savory and herb-infused marinade.

Lemon Garlic Herb Marinade Recipe

Ingredients:

- Zest and juice of 2 lemons
- 4 cloves garlic, minced

- 2 tablespoons fresh parsley, finely chopped
- 1 tablespoon fresh thyme leaves, chopped
- 1 tablespoon fresh rosemary leaves, finely chopped
- 1/4 cup olive oil
- 1/2 teaspoon kosher salt
- 1/4 teaspoon black pepper

Instructions:

1. In a mixing bowl, combine the zest and juice of 2 lemons, minced garlic, finely chopped fresh parsley, chopped fresh thyme leaves, finely chopped fresh rosemary leaves, olive oil, kosher salt, and black pepper.

2. Stir the ingredients together until they are well combined, creating a flavorful Lemon Garlic Herb Marinade.

3. Taste the marinade and adjust the level of herbiness or acidity by adding more fresh herbs or lemon juice to suit your preference.

4. Transfer the Lemon Garlic Herb Marinade to an airtight container or a glass jar with a tight-fitting lid. Store it in the refrigerator until ready to use.

Suggested Uses for Lemon Garlic Herb Marinade:

1. Lemon Garlic Herb Marinated Chicken: Marinate chicken pieces in the Lemon Garlic Herb Marinade before grilling, baking, or pan-searing for a fresh and herbaceous dish.

2. Lemon Garlic Herb Marinated Shrimp: Season shrimp with the marinade before grilling, sautéing, or skewering for a citrusy and aromatic seafood dish.

3. Lemon Garlic Herb Roasted Vegetables: Toss a mix of vegetables like asparagus, bell peppers, and red onions in the marinade before roasting for a fragrant and herb-infused side dish.

4. Lemon Garlic Herb Marinated Tofu: Coat tofu cubes with the marinade before grilling, pan-frying, or baking for a vegetarian option.

5. Lemon Garlic Herb Salad Dressing: Use the marinade as a dressing for salads with mixed greens, cherry tomatoes, and croutons.

The Lemon Garlic Herb Marinade combines the zesty freshness of lemon with the aromatic and savory notes of garlic and herbs. It's a versatile marinade that adds a burst of citrus and herbaceous flavor to your dishes, making it a flavorful addition to your culinary repertoire. Enjoy experimenting with different recipes to showcase the deliciousness of this bright and flavorful marinade.

Cuban Mojo Marinade Recipe

Ingredients:

- Zest and juice of 3 oranges

- Zest and juice of 3 limes

- 6 cloves garlic, minced

- 1/4 cup fresh cilantro, finely chopped

- 1/4 cup fresh mint leaves, finely chopped

- 1/4 cup olive oil

- 1 teaspoon ground cumin

- 1 teaspoon dried oregano

- 1 teaspoon kosher salt

- 1/2 teaspoon black pepper

Instructions:

1.   In a mixing bowl, combine the zest and juice of 3 oranges, the zest and juice of 3 limes, minced garlic, finely chopped fresh cilantro, finely chopped fresh mint leaves, olive oil, ground cumin, dried oregano, kosher salt, and black pepper.

2.   Stir the ingredients together until they are well combined, creating a flavorful Cuban Mojo Marinade.

3.   Taste the marinade and adjust the citrusy brightness or herbiness level by adding more citrus juice or fresh herbs to suit your preference.

4.   Transfer the Cuban Mojo Marinade to an airtight container or a glass jar with a tight-fitting lid. Store it in the refrigerator until ready to use.

Suggested Uses for Cuban Mojo Marinade:

1.   Cuban Mojo Marinated Pork: Marinate pork shoulder or tenderloin in the Cuban Mojo Marinade before slow-roasting or grilling for an authentic Cuban dish.

2.   Cuban Mojo Marinated Chicken: Season chicken pieces with the mari- nade before grilling, baking, or pan-searing for a zesty and citrusy dish.

3.   Cuban Mojo Marinated Tofu: Use the marinade to marinate and grill tofu for a vegetarian take on Cuban flavors.

4.   Cuban Mojo Roasted Vegetables: Toss vegetables like bell peppers, onions, and sweet potatoes in the marinade before roasting for a vibrant and flavorful side dish.

5.   Cuban Mojo Rice and Beans: Use the marinade as a seasoning for cooking rice and black beans for a traditional Cuban side dish.

The Cuban Mojo Marinade combines the bright and citrusy notes of oranges and limes with the aromatic flavors of garlic, cilantro, and mint. It's a versatile marinade that brings the authentic taste of Cuban cuisine to your dishes, making it a flavorful addition to your culinary repertoire. Enjoy experimenting with different recipes to showcase the deliciousness of this vibrant and zesty marinade.

Sriracha Lime Marinade Recipe

Ingredients:

- Zest and juice of 3 limes

- 3 tablespoons Sriracha sauce (adjust to taste)

- 2 cloves garlic, minced

- 2 tablespoons honey

- 2 tablespoons soy sauce

- 2 tablespoons olive oil

- 1/2 teaspoon kosher salt

- 1/4 teaspoon black pepper

Instructions:

1. In a mixing bowl, combine the zest and juice of 3 limes, Sriracha sauce (adjust to your preferred level of spiciness), minced garlic, honey, soy sauce, olive oil, kosher salt, and black pepper.

2. Stir the ingredients together until they are well combined, creating a flavorful Sriracha Lime Marinade.

3. Taste the marinade and adjust the level of spiciness or sweetness by adding more Sriracha sauce or honey to suit your preference.

4. Transfer the Sriracha Lime Marinade to an airtight container or a glass jar with a tight-fitting lid. Store it in the refrigerator until ready to use.

Suggested Uses for Sriracha Lime Marinade:

1. Sriracha Lime Marinated Chicken: Marinate chicken pieces in the Sriracha Lime Marinade before grilling, baking, or pan-searing for a spicy and zesty dish.

2. Sriracha Lime Marinated Shrimp: Season shrimp with the marinade before grilling, sautéing, or skewering for a fiery and citrusy seafood dish.

3. Sriracha Lime Marinated Tofu: Coat tofu cubes with the marinade before grilling, pan-frying, or baking for a vegetarian option.

4. Sriracha Lime Stir-Fry: Use the marinade as a sauce for stir-frying a mix of vegetables, protein, and cooked rice or noodles.

5. Sriracha Lime Salad Dressing: Use the marinade as a dressing for salads with mixed greens, cherry tomatoes, and avocado.

The Sriracha Lime Marinade combines the heat of Sriracha sauce with the zesty brightness of lime juice. It's a versatile marinade that adds a spicy and tangy kick to your dishes, making it a flavorful addition to your culinary repertoire. Enjoy experimenting with different recipes to showcase the deliciousness of this spicy and citrusy marinade.

Hawaiian Huli Huli Marinade Recipe

Ingredients:

- 1 cup pineapple juice

- 1/2 cup soy sauce

- 1/4 cup brown sugar

- 1/4 cup ketchup

- 1/4 cup rice vinegar

- 2 cloves garlic, minced

- 1 tablespoon fresh ginger, minced

- 1/2 teaspoon ground cinnamon

- 1/2 teaspoon ground paprika

- 1/4 teaspoon black pepper

Instructions:

1. In a mixing bowl, combine the pineapple juice, soy sauce, brown sugar, ketchup, rice vinegar, minced garlic, minced fresh ginger, ground cinnamon, ground paprika, and black pepper.

2. Stir the ingredients together until they are well combined, creating a flavorful Hawaiian Huli Huli Marinade.

3. Taste the marinade and adjust the level of sweetness or spiciness by adding more brown sugar or black pepper to suit your preference.

4. Transfer the Hawaiian Huli Huli Marinade to an airtight container or a glass jar with a tight-fitting lid. Store it in the refrigerator until ready to use.

Suggested Uses for Hawaiian Huli Huli Marinade:

1. Hawaiian Huli Huli Grilled Chicken: Marinate chicken pieces in the Hawaiian Huli Huli Marinade before grilling for a sweet and savory dish reminiscent of Hawaiian flavors.

2. Hawaiian Huli Huli Marinated Pork: Season pork chops or tenderloin with the marinade before grilling or roasting for a tropical and flavorful meat dish.

3. Hawaiian Huli Huli Tofu Skewers: Use the marinade to marinate and grill tofu skewers for a vegetarian twist on Hawaiian cuisine.

4. Hawaiian Huli Huli Glazed Salmon: Use the marinade as a glaze for baked or grilled salmon fillets.

5. Hawaiian Huli Huli Stir-Fry: Use the marinade as a sauce for stir-frying a mix of vegetables, protein, and cooked rice or noodles.

The Hawaiian Huli Huli Marinade combines the sweetness of pineapple juice with the umami richness of soy sauce and the aromatic flavors of garlic and ginger. It's a versatile marinade that brings the tropical taste of Hawaii to your dishes, making it a flavorful addition to your culinary repertoire. Enjoy experimenting with different recipes to showcase the deliciousness of this sweet and savory marinade.

Balsamic Fig Marinade Recipe

Ingredients:

·   1/2 cup balsamic vinegar

·   1/4 cup extra-virgin olive oil

·   1/4 cup fig preserves or fig jam

·   2 cloves garlic, minced

·   1 teaspoon Dijon mustard

·   1 teaspoon fresh rosemary leaves, finely chopped

·   1/2 teaspoon kosher salt

·   1/4 teaspoon black pepper

Instructions:

1.   Combine the balsamic vinegar, extra-virgin olive oil, fig preserves or fig jam, minced garlic, Dijon mustard, finely chopped fresh rosemary leaves, kosher salt, and black pepper in a mixing bowl.

2.   Stir the ingredients together until they are well combined, creating a flavorful Balsamic Fig Marinade.

3.   Taste the marinade and adjust the level of sweetness or herbiness by adding more fig preserves or fresh rosemary to suit your preference.

4.   Transfer the Balsamic Fig Marinade to an airtight container or a glass jar with a tight-fitting lid. Store it in the refrigerator until ready to use.

Suggested Uses for Balsamic Fig Marinade:

1.   Balsamic Fig Marinated Chicken: Marinate chicken pieces in the Bal- samic Fig Marinade before grilling, baking, or pan-searing for a sweet and savory dish.

2.   Balsamic Fig Marinated Pork: Season pork chops or tenderloin with the marinade before grilling or roasting for a flavorful, fruity meat dish.

3.   Balsamic Fig Marinated Salmon: Use the marinade as a glaze for baked or grilled salmon fillets.

4.   Balsamic Fig Roasted Vegetables: Toss a mix of vegetables like Brussels sprouts, carrots, and red onions in the marinade before roasting for a sweet and herb-infused side dish.

5.   Balsamic Fig Salad Dressing: Use the marinade as a dressing for salads with mixed greens, goat cheese, candied pecans, and fresh figs.

The Balsamic Fig Marinade combines the rich and tangy flavors of balsamic vinegar with the sweetness of fig preserves and the aromatic notes of rosemary. It's a versatile marinade that adds a delightful fruity and herbaceous touch to your dishes, making it a flavorful addition to your culinary repertoire. Enjoy experimenting with different recipes to showcase the deliciousness of this sweet and savory marinade.

Miso Orange Marinade Recipe

Ingredients:

·   1/4 cup white miso paste

·   Zest and juice of 2 oranges

·   2 tablespoons honey

·   2 cloves garlic, minced

·   1 tablespoon fresh ginger, minced

·   2 tablespoons soy sauce

·   2 tablespoons rice vinegar

·   1/4 teaspoon black pepper

Instructions:

1.   In a mixing bowl, combine the white miso paste, zest, and juice of 2 oranges, honey, minced garlic, minced fresh ginger, soy sauce, rice vinegar, and black pepper.

2.   Stir the ingredients together until they are well combined, creating a flavorful Miso Orange Marinade.

3.   Taste the marinade and adjust the level of sweetness or saltiness by adding more honey or soy sauce to suit your preference.

4.   Transfer the Miso Orange Marinade to an airtight container or a glass jar with a tight-fitting lid. Store it in the refrigerator until ready to use.

Suggested Uses for Miso Orange Marinade:

1.   Miso Orange Marinated Chicken: Marinate chicken pieces in the Miso Orange Marinade before grilling, baking, or pan-searing for a sweet and savory dish.

2.   Miso Orange Marinated Salmon: Season salmon fillets with the mari- nade before grilling, roasting, or pan-searing for a flavorful seafood dish.

3.   Miso Orange Marinated Tofu: Coat tofu cubes with the marinade before grilling, pan-frying, or baking for a vegetarian option.

4.   Miso Orange Stir-Fry: Use the marinade as a sauce for stir-frying a mix of vegetables, protein, and cooked rice or noodles.

5.   Miso Orange Glazed Vegetables: Use the marinade as a glaze for roasted or grilled vegetables like asparagus, bell peppers, and zucchini.

The Miso Orange Marinade combines the savory richness of white miso paste with the citrusy brightness of orange juice and zest. It's a versatile marinade that adds a delightful sweet and umami flavor profile to your dishes, making it a flavorful addition to your culinary repertoire. Enjoy experimenting with different recipes to showcase the deliciousness of this unique and flavorful marinade.

Garlic Cilantro Lime Marinade Recipe

Ingredients:

·   Zest and juice of 4 limes

·   6 cloves garlic, minced

·   1/4 cup fresh cilantro leaves, finely chopped

·   1/4 cup olive oil

·   1 teaspoon ground cumin

·   1 teaspoon ground coriander

·   1/2 teaspoon kosher salt

·   1/4 teaspoon black pepper

Instructions:

1.   In a mixing bowl, combine the zest and juice of 4 limes, minced garlic, finely chopped fresh cilantro leaves, olive oil, ground cumin, ground coriander, kosher salt, and black pepper.

2.   Stir the ingredients together until they are well combined, creating a flavorful Garlic Cilantro Lime Marinade.

3.   Taste the marinade and adjust the level of herbiness or acidity by adding more fresh cilantro or lime juice to suit your preference.

4.   Transfer the Garlic Cilantro Lime Marinade to an airtight container or a glass jar with a tight-fitting lid. Store it in the refrigerator until ready to use.

Suggested Uses for Garlic Cilantro Lime Marinade:

1.   Garlic Cilantro Lime Marinated Chicken: Marinate chicken pieces in the Garlic Cilantro Lime Marinade before grilling, baking, or pan-searing for a zesty and herbaceous dish.

2.   Garlic Cilantro Lime Marinated Shrimp: Season shrimp with the mari- nade before grilling, sautéing, or skewering for a citrusy and aromatic seafood dish.

3.   Garlic Cilantro Lime Marinated Steak: Use the marinade to marinate steak cuts before grilling or broiling for a flavorful

and zesty meat dish.

4.   Garlic Cilantro Lime Grilled Vegetables: Toss vegetables like bell peppers, zucchini, and red onion in the marinade before grilling for a vibrant and herb-infused side dish.

5.   Garlic Cilantro Lime Salad Dressing: Use the marinade as a dressing for salads with mixed greens, cherry tomatoes, black beans, and avocado.

The Garlic Cilantro Lime Marinade combines the zesty brightness of lime with the aromatic notes of garlic and cilantro. It's a versatile marinade that adds a burst of citrus and herbaceous flavor to your dishes, making it a flavorful addition to your culinary repertoire. Enjoy experimenting with different recipes to showcase the deliciousness of this zesty and herb-infused marinade.

Herb Butter Marinade Recipe

Ingredients:

·   1/2 cup unsalted butter, melted

·   2 cloves garlic, minced

·   2 tablespoons fresh parsley, finely chopped

·   2 tablespoons fresh thyme leaves, chopped

·   2 tablespoons fresh rosemary leaves, finely chopped

·   1/2 teaspoon kosher salt

·   1/4 teaspoon black pepper

Instructions:

1.   Combine the melted unsalted butter, minced garlic, finely chopped fresh parsley, chopped fresh thyme leaves, finely chopped fresh rosemary leaves, kosher salt, and black pepper in a mixing bowl.

2.   Stir the ingredients together until they are well combined, creating a flavorful Herb Butter Marinade.

3.   Taste the marinade and adjust the level of herbiness or saltiness by adding more fresh herbs or salt to suit your preference.

4.   Transfer the Herb Butter Marinade to an airtight container or a glass jar with a tight-fitting lid. Store it in the refrigerator until ready to use.

Suggested Uses for Herb Butter Marinade:

1.   Herb Butter Marinated Steak: Brush steak cuts with the Herb Butter Marinade before grilling or broiling for a rich and herb-infused meat dish.

2.   Herb Butter Marinated Grilled Vegetables: Use the marinade to coat vegetables like asparagus, mushrooms, and corn before grilling for a flavorful and buttery side dish.

3.   Herb Butter Roasted Chicken: Rub the marinade under the skin and all over a whole chicken before roasting for a juicy and herb-infused poultry dish.

4.   Herb Butter Marinated Shrimp: Toss shrimp in the marinade before skewering and grilling for a delectable seafood dish.

5.   Herb Butter Spread: Melt the Herb Butter Marinade and use it as a spread for bread or rolls or as a topping for baked potatoes.

The Herb Butter Marinade combines the richness of melted butter with the aromatic flavors of garlic and fresh herbs. It's a versatile marinade that adds a decadent and herbaceous touch to your dishes, making it a flavorful addition to your culinary repertoire. Enjoy experimenting with different recipes to showcase the deliciousness of this savory and buttery marinade.

Coconut Curry Marinade Recipe

Ingredients:

·   1 cup canned coconut milk

·   2 tablespoons red curry paste

·   2 cloves garlic, minced

·   1 tablespoon fresh ginger, minced

·   2 tablespoons soy sauce

·   2 tablespoons brown sugar

·   1 tablespoon lime juice

·   1/2 teaspoon turmeric powder

·   1/2 teaspoon kosher salt

·   1/4 teaspoon black pepper

Instructions:

1.   Combine the canned coconut milk, red curry paste, minced garlic, fresh ginger, soy sauce, brown sugar, lime juice, turmeric powder, kosher salt, and black pepper in a mixing bowl.

2.   Stir the ingredients together until they are well combined, creating a flavorful Coconut Curry Marinade.

3.   Taste the marinade and adjust the level of spiciness or sweetness by adding more red curry paste or brown sugar to suit your preference.

4.   Transfer the Coconut Curry Marinade to an airtight container or a glass jar with a tight-fitting lid. Store it in the refrigerator until ready to use.

Suggested Uses for Coconut Curry Marinade:

1.   Coconut Curry Marinated Chicken: Marinate chicken pieces in the Coconut Curry Marinade before grilling, baking, or pan-searing for a rich and flavorful dish.

2.   Coconut Curry Marinated Tofu: Coat tofu cubes with the marinade before grilling, pan-frying, or baking for a vegetarian option.

3.   Coconut Curry Marinated Shrimp: Season shrimp with the marinade before grilling, sautéing, or skewering for a creamy and spicy seafood dish.

4.   Coconut Curry Stir-Fry: Use the marinade as a sauce for stir-frying a mix of vegetables, protein, and cooked rice or noodles.

5.   Coconut Curry Sauce: Simmer the marinade with additional coconut milk and a splash of chicken or vegetable broth to create a creamy and aromatic curry sauce for serving with rice or noodles.

The Coconut Curry Marinade combines the creamy richness of coconut milk with the bold and spicy flavors of red curry paste. It's a versatile marinade that adds a delightful creaminess and spiciness to your dishes, making it a flavorful addition to your culinary repertoire. Enjoy experimenting with different recipes to showcase the deliciousness of this coconut curry-infused marinade.

Spicy Mango Marinade Recipe

Ingredients:

- 1 ripe mango, peeled and diced
- 2 tablespoons chili paste (adjust to taste)
- 2 cloves garlic, minced
- 1 tablespoon fresh ginger, minced
- 1/4 cup rice vinegar
- 2 tablespoons soy sauce
- 2 tablespoons honey
- 1/2 teaspoon kosher salt
- 1/4 teaspoon black pepper

Instructions:

1.   In a blender or food processor, combine the diced ripe mango, chili paste (adjust to your preferred level of spiciness), minced garlic, minced fresh ginger, rice vinegar, soy sauce, honey, kosher salt, and black pepper.

2.   Blend the ingredients until you have a smooth and uniform mixture, creating a flavorful Spicy Mango Marinade.

3.   Taste the marinade and adjust the level of spiciness or sweetness by adding more chili paste or honey to suit your preference.

4.   Transfer the Spicy Mango Marinade to an airtight container or a glass jar with a tight-fitting lid. Store it in the refrigerator until ready to use.

Suggested Uses for Spicy Mango Marinade:

1.   Spicy Mango Marinated Chicken: Marinate chicken pieces in the Spicy Mango Marinade before grilling, baking, or pan-searing for a fruity and spicy dish.

2.   Spicy Mango Marinated Shrimp: Season shrimp with the marinade before grilling, sautéing, or skewering for a fiery and tropical seafood dish.

3.   Spicy Mango Marinated Tofu: Use the marinade to marinate and grill tofu for a vegetarian option with a kick.

4.   Spicy Mango Glazed Pork: Brush the marinade on pork chops or tenderloin before grilling or roasting for a sweet and spicy meat dish.

5.   Spicy Mango Salad Dressing: Use the marinade as a dressing for salads with mixed greens, grilled chicken, avocado, and red onion.

The Spicy Mango Marinade combines the sweetness of ripe mango with the heat of chili paste and the aromatic notes of garlic and ginger. It's a versatile marinade that adds a fruity and spicy kick to your dishes, making it a flavorful addition to your culinary repertoire. Enjoy experimenting with different recipes to showcase the deliciousness of this tropical and fiery marinade.

Sundried Tomato Pesto Marinade Recipe

Ingredients:

- 1/2 cup sundried tomatoes (dry or packed in oil), drained

- 1/4 cup fresh basil leaves

- 2 cloves garlic

- 1/4 cup grated Parmesan cheese

- 1/4 cup pine nuts

- 1/4 cup extra-virgin olive oil

- 1 tablespoon lemon juice

- 1/2 teaspoon kosher salt

- 1/4 teaspoon black pepper

Instructions:

1.   Combine the sundried tomatoes, fresh basil leaves, minced garlic, grated Parmesan cheese, pine nuts, extra-virgin olive oil, lemon juice, kosher salt, and black pepper in a food processor or blender.

2.	Blend the ingredients until you have a smooth and vibrant mixture, creating a flavorful Sundried Tomato Pesto Marinade.

3.	Taste the marinade and adjust the level of saltiness or acidity by adding more Parmesan cheese or lemon juice to suit your preference.

4.	Transfer the Sundried Tomato Pesto Marinade to an airtight container or a glass jar with a tight-fitting lid. Store it in the refrigerator until ready to use.

Suggested Uses for Sundried Tomato Pesto Marinade:

1.	Sundried Tomato Pesto Marinated Chicken: Marinate chicken pieces in the Sundried Tomato Pesto Marinade before grilling, baking, or pan- searing for a flavorful and Mediterranean-inspired dish.

2.	Sundried Tomato Pesto Marinated Shrimp: Season shrimp with the marinade before grilling, sautéing, or skewering for a tangy and aromatic seafood dish.

3.	Sundried Tomato Pesto Marinated Vegetables: Toss vegetables like cherry tomatoes, zucchini, and bell peppers in the marinade before roasting for a vibrant and herb-infused side dish.

4.	Sundried Tomato Pesto Pasta: Use the marinade as a sauce for tossing with cooked pasta, adding in some fresh basil and grated Parmesan cheese.

5.	Sundried Tomato Pesto Pizza: Spread the marinade on pizza dough, add mozzarella cheese, and top with your favorite pizza ingredients before baking for a unique and flavorful pizza.

The Sundried Tomato Pesto Marinade combines the intense flavor of sundried tomatoes with the freshness of basil and the richness of Parmesan cheese. It's a versatile marinade that adds a burst of Mediterranean-inspired taste to your dishes, making it a flavorful addition to your culinary repertoire. Enjoy experimenting with different recipes to showcase the deliciousness of this tangy and aromatic marinade.

Lemon Basil Marinade Recipe

Ingredients:

·	Zest and juice of 3 lemons

·	1/2 cup fresh basil leaves, finely chopped

·	3 cloves garlic, minced

·	1/4 cup extra-virgin olive oil

·	2 tablespoons honey

·	1/2 teaspoon kosher salt

·	1/4 teaspoon black pepper

Instructions:

1.   Combine the zest and juice of 3 lemons, finely chopped fresh basil leaves, minced garlic, extra-virgin olive oil, honey, kosher salt, and black pepper in a mixing bowl.

2.   Stir the ingredients together until they are well combined, creating a flavorful Lemon Basil Marinade.

3.   Taste the marinade and adjust the level of sweetness or acidity by adding more honey or lemon juice to suit your preference.

4.   Transfer the Lemon Basil Marinade to an airtight container or a glass jar with a tight-fitting lid. Store it in the refrigerator until ready to use.

Suggested Uses for Lemon Basil Marinade:

1.   Lemon Basil Marinated Chicken: Marinate chicken pieces in the Lemon Basil Marinade before grilling, baking, or pan-searing for a zesty and herbaceous dish.

2.   Lemon Basil Marinated Shrimp: Season shrimp with the marinade before grilling, sautéing, or skewering for a citrusy and aromatic seafood dish.

3.   Lemon Basil Marinated Vegetables: Toss vegetables like asparagus, cherry tomatoes, and yellow squash in the marinade before grilling or roasting for a fresh and herb-infused side dish.

4.   Lemon Basil Salad Dressing: Use the marinade as a dressing for salads with mixed greens, fresh mozzarella, sun-dried tomatoes, and pine nuts.

5.   Lemon Basil Quinoa: Mix the marinade with cooked quinoa and chopped vegetables for a flavorful and refreshing quinoa salad.

The Lemon Basil Marinade combines the bright and zesty flavor of lemon with the fresh aroma of basil. It's a versatile marinade that adds a burst of citrus and herbaceous taste to your dishes, making it a flavorful addition to your culinary repertoire. Enjoy experimenting with different recipes to showcase the deliciousness of this zesty and herb-infused marinade.

5
Elevating Sauces

The World of Sauces

Sauces are the unsung heroes of the culinary world, adding depth, flavor, and elegance to dishes across cultures and cuisines. They are the magical finishing touches that can transform a simple meal into a gourmet experience. This chapter delves into the fascinating world of sauces, exploring their history, significance, and versatility.

The Significance of Sauces:

- Sauces have been integral to culinary traditions for centuries, dating back to ancient civilizations.

- They are often used to balance flavors, add moisture, and provide a harmonious contrast to the main ingredients.

- Sauces can be the defining element of a dish, making it unique and memorable.

Types of Sauces

(Classic, Gravies, Vinaigrettes, and More)

Sauces come in a wide array of styles and flavors, each serving a distinct purpose in the culinary landscape. Understanding the various types of sauces empowers cooks to create dishes with exceptional taste and presentation.

1.   Classic Sauces:

- Classic sauces include the five mother sauces of French cuisine: Béchamel, Velouté, Espagnole (Brown), Tomato, and Hollandaise. These serve as the foundation for countless derivative sauces.

2.   Gravies:

- Gravies are often made from pan drippings, stock, and a thickening agent like flour or cornstarch. They are commonly served with roasted meats and poultry.

3.   Vinaigrettes:

- Vinaigrettes are emulsified dressings made from oil, vinegar, and season- ings. They are used to flavor salads and mari- nate vegetables, meats, or seafood.

4.   Salsas:

- Salsas are typically tomato-based sauces with various seasonings, includ- ing onions, garlic, chilies, and herbs. They are a staple in Latin American and Mexican cuisines.

5.   Pesto:

- Pesto is a vibrant sauce originating from Italy, traditionally made with basil, pine nuts, garlic, Parmesan cheese, and olive oil. It is often served with pasta or used as a spread.

6.   Reduction Sauces:

·   Reduction sauces are made by simmering liquids (wine, stock, or juices) to concentrate flavors. They are often drizzled over meats and fish.

7.   Cream Sauces:

·   Cream sauces are made by combining cream or milk with flavorings like mushrooms, cheese, or herbs. They are velvety and luxurious additions to dishes.

Enhancing Dishes with Sauces

Sauces play a crucial role in enhancing the overall dining experience. They can add complexity, contrast, and depth of flavor to a wide range of dishes. Understanding how to pair sauces with ingredients is key to elevating your culinary creations.

Pairing Considerations:

·   Balance acidity with richness: Creamy sauces can complement acidic ingredients like tomatoes or citrus.

·   Contrast textures: A crispy protein can benefit from a velvety sauce, while a tender, slow-cooked dish might pair well with a vibrant, chunky salsa.

·   Highlight flavors: Match the sauce to the dominant flavors in your dish, whether they are sweet, savory, or spicy.

Popular Sauce Recipes

Classic Sauces

Béarnaise Sauce Recipe

Ingredients:

·   2 tablespoons white wine vinegar

·   2 tablespoons dry white wine

·   2 tablespoons minced shallots

·   2 tablespoons fresh tarragon leaves, chopped

·   3 large egg yolks

·   1/2 cup (1 stick) unsalted butter, melted and clarified

·   Salt and white pepper to taste

·   Cayenne pepper (optional, for a hint of heat)

Instructions:

1. Begin by preparing a reduction. In a small saucepan, combine the white wine vinegar, dry white wine, minced shallots, and half of the chopped fresh tarragon leaves. Heat over medium heat until the mixture reduces by half, approximately 5-7 minutes. Remove from heat and allow it to cool slightly.

2. In a separate heatproof bowl, whisk the egg yolks until they become pale and slightly thickened.

3. Gradually drizzle the melted and clarified butter into the egg yolks while continuously whisking. Add the butter slowly to prevent curdling, and continue whisking until the mixture emulsifies and thickens.

4. Strain the reduced vinegar and wine mixture into the bowl with the egg yolk and butter mixture. This step removes the shallot and tarragon pieces. Stir well to combine.

5. Place the bowl over a pot of simmering water (double boiler) and continue to whisk the mixture until it thickens to a sauce-like consistency. This should take about 5-7 minutes. Be cautious not to overheat, as it can cause the sauce to curdle.

6. Remove the sauce from heat and add the remaining chopped fresh tarragon. Season the Béarnaise Sauce with salt and white pepper to taste. If desired, add a pinch of cayenne pepper for a hint of heat.

7. Taste the sauce and adjust the seasoning or herb flavors as needed.

8. Serve the Béarnaise Sauce immediately as a luxurious topping for grilled steak, poached eggs, or grilled vegetables.

Suggested Uses for Béarnaise Sauce:

1. Steak Topping: Drizzle it over perfectly grilled steaks to enhance their flavor and richness.

2. Poached Eggs: Serve it over poached eggs for a classic Eggs Benedict.

3. Grilled Chicken: Elevate grilled chicken breasts or thighs by spooning Béarnaise Sauce on top.

4. Vegetable Dip: Use it as a dip for blanched or roasted vegetables for a gourmet touch.

5. Seafood: Pair it with seafood like grilled shrimp or lobster for an indulgent seafood experience.

Béarnaise Sauce is a velvety and flavorful classic that elevates a wide range of dishes, especially grilled meats and eggs. Its versatility makes it a favorite among chefs and food enthusiasts alike. Enjoy the culinary luxury of homemade Béarnaise Sauce in your kitchen creations.

Velouté Sauce Recipe

Ingredients:

- 2 cups chicken or vegetable broth

- 2 tablespoons unsalted butter

- 2 tablespoons all-purpose flour

- Salt and white pepper to taste

·   Pinch of ground nutmeg (optional)

Instructions:

1.   Start by heating the chicken or vegetable broth in a saucepan until it's hot but not boiling. Keep it warm on the stovetop.

2.   In a separate saucepan, melt the unsalted butter over medium heat.

3.   Add the all-purpose flour to the melted butter, and continuously whisk to create a smooth paste. This mixture is known as a "roux."

4.   Cook the roux, stirring constantly, for about 2-3 minutes until it turns a light, pale color. Be careful not to let it brown.

5.   Gradually and slowly add the hot broth to the roux while whisking vigorously to prevent lumps from forming. Continue adding the broth until the mixture is smooth and thoroughly combined.

6.   Bring the sauce to a simmer and cook for approximately 10-15 minutes, stirring frequently, until it thickens and reaches a velvety consistency. The sauce should coat the back of a spoon.

7.   Season the Velouté Sauce with salt and white pepper to taste. If desired, add a pinch of ground nutmeg for extra flavor. Taste and adjust the seasoning as needed.

8.   Once the Velouté Sauce is ready, remove it from the heat and use it immediately as a base for other sauces or as a creamy addition to various dishes.

Variations and Uses for Velouté Sauce:

1.   Suprême Sauce: Incorporate heavy cream, lemon juice, and finely chopped mushrooms into the Velouté Sauce for a Suprême Sauce that pairs well with poultry dishes.

2.   Normande Sauce: Combine Velouté Sauce with heavy cream, egg yolks, and diced apples or applesauce for a Normande Sauce that complements seafood dishes.

3.   Poulette Sauce: Mix Velouté Sauce with heavy cream, chopped parsley, and lemon juice to create a Poulette Sauce perfect for chicken or seafood.

4.   Mushroom Velouté: Sauté finely chopped mushrooms in butter until they release their moisture, and then add them to the Velouté Sauce for a rich and earthy Mushroom Velouté.

5.   Seafood Velouté: Use fish or seafood broth instead of chicken or vegetable broth to make a Seafood Velouté, ideal for seafood dishes.

Velouté Sauce is a versatile base sauce that forms the foundation for many classic sauces. Its adaptability makes it an essential component in the culinary world, allowing it to enhance a wide range of recipes and cuisines. Enjoy the flexibility and richness of homemade Velouté Sauce in your cooking endeavors.

Espagnole Sauce (Brown Sauce) Recipe

Ingredients:

- 2 tablespoons unsalted butter
- 2 tablespoons all-purpose flour
- 1/2 cup finely chopped onion
- 1/4 cup finely chopped carrot
- 1/4 cup finely chopped celery
- 1 clove garlic, minced
- 2 cups beef or veal stock
- 1/4 cup tomato paste
- 1 bay leaf
- 4-5 black peppercorns
- Salt and black pepper to taste

Instructions:

1. In a saucepan, melt the unsalted butter over medium heat.

2. Add the finely chopped onion, carrot, and celery to the melted butter. Sauté the vegetables until they become tender and start to brown, about 10 minutes.

3. Stir in the minced garlic and cook for an additional 1-2 minutes until fragrant.

4. Sprinkle the all-purpose flour over the sautéed vegetables and continue to cook, stirring constantly, for about 5 minutes. The flour should take on a light brown color and create a thick paste, known as a "roux."

5. Gradually add the beef or veal stock to the roux, whisking vigorously to prevent lumps from forming. Continue to whisk until the mixture is smooth and well combined.

6. Stir in the tomato paste, bay leaf, and black peppercorns.

7. Bring the sauce to a simmer, then reduce the heat to low. Let it gently simmer for approximately 30-45 minutes, allowing it to thicken and develop flavors. Stir occasionally.

8. Taste the Espagnole Sauce and season with salt and black pepper to taste. Remove and discard the bay leaf and peppercorns.

9. Strain the sauce through a fine-mesh sieve or cheesecloth to remove any remaining solids, resulting in a smooth and velvety texture.

10. Your Espagnole Sauce (Brown Sauce) is now ready to be used as a base for other sauces or as a rich addition to various dishes.

Suggested Uses for Espagnole Sauce:

1. Demiglace Sauce: Reduce Espagnole Sauce further to create a demiglace, which is an intensely flavorful sauce used in gourmet dishes.

2. Mushroom Sauce: Add sautéed mushrooms, shallots, and a splash of red wine to Espagnole Sauce for a savory mushroom sauce.

3.   Bordelaise Sauce: Enhance it with red wine, shallots, and bone marrow for a classic Bordelaise Sauce that pairs beautifully with steak.

4.   Hunter's Sauce (Chasseur Sauce): Combine Espagnole Sauce with mushrooms, tomatoes, white wine, and herbs for a delightful Hunter's Sauce.

5.   Meat Dishes: Use it as a rich and savory sauce for beef, veal, or game meats.

Espagnole Sauce, also known as Brown Sauce, is a foundational sauce in French cuisine. It serves as a versatile base for various sauces and can elevate the flavors of meat dishes. Enjoy the depth and complexity of homemade Espagnole Sauce in your culinary creations.

Hollandaise Sauce Recipe

Ingredients:

·   3 large egg yolks

·   1 tablespoon fresh lemon juice

·   1/2 cup (1 stick) unsalted butter, melted and clarified

·   Pinch of cayenne pepper (optional)

·   Pinch of salt

Instructions:

1.   In a heatproof bowl, whisk the egg yolks and fresh lemon juice together until they are well combined.

2.   Place the bowl over a pot of simmering water (double boiler). Ensure that the bottom of the bowl doesn't touch the water.

3.   While continuously whisking, slowly drizzle in the melted and clarified butter. Add it gradually to prevent the sauce from breaking.

4.   Continue to whisk the mixture until it thickens and becomes smooth and creamy. This should take about 5-7 minutes.

5.   If desired, add a pinch of cayenne pepper for a hint of heat and a pinch of salt for seasoning. Whisk to combine.

6.   Remove the Hollandaise Sauce from the heat and serve it immediately as a luxurious topping or accompaniment.

Suggested Uses for Hollandaise Sauce:

1.   Eggs Benedict: Pour Hollandaise Sauce over poached eggs and Canadian bacon on English muffins for the classic Eggs Benedict.

2.   Asparagus: Drizzle it over blanched or grilled asparagus spears as a flavorful side dish.

3.   Salmon: Serve it as a rich, creamy sauce with grilled or poached salmon fillets.

4.   Vegetables: Use it as a sauce for steamed or roasted vegetables, such as broccoli or Brussels sprouts.

5.   Steak: Elevate your steak by spooning Hollandaise Sauce on top for a decadent twist.

Hollandaise Sauce is a creamy, buttery classic French sauce that adds richness to various dishes. Its velvety texture and tangy flavor make it a versatile condiment that can be enjoyed in both breakfast and dinner recipes. Experi- ment with these suggested uses to experience the luxuriousness of homemade Hollandaise Sauce.

Tomato Marinara Sauce Recipe

Ingredients:

·   2 tablespoons olive oil

·   1 small onion, finely chopped

·   2 cloves garlic, minced

·   1 (28-ounce) can crushed tomatoes

·   1 (14-ounce) can diced tomatoes

·   2 teaspoons dried basil

·   1 teaspoon dried oregano

·   1/2 teaspoon red pepper flakes (adjust to taste)

·   Salt and black pepper to taste

·   1 tablespoon sugar (optional, to balance acidity)

Instructions:

1.   In a large saucepan, heat the olive oil over medium heat.

2.   Add the finely chopped onion and sauté for about 5 minutes until it becomes translucent and soft.

3.   Stir in the minced garlic and cook for an additional 1-2 minutes until fragrant. Be careful not to let it brown.

4.   Add the crushed tomatoes and diced tomatoes (with their juices) to the saucepan and stir to combine.

5.   Season the sauce with dried basil, dried oregano, red pepper flakes (adjust to your preferred level of spiciness), salt, and black pepper. If the tomatoes are too acidic, you can add a tablespoon of sugar to balance the flavors.

6.   Bring the sauce to a simmer, then reduce the heat to low. Let it gently simmer, uncovered, for about 20-30 minutes, stirring occasionally. This allows the flavors to meld, and the sauce will thicken.

7.   Taste the Tomato Marinara Sauce and adjust the seasonings as needed. If you prefer a smoother texture, you can use an immersion blender to blend the sauce until it reaches your desired consistency.

8.   Remove the sauce from heat and use it immediately as a pasta sauce, pizza sauce, or other Italian dish.

Suggested Uses for Tomato Marinara Sauce:

1.   Pasta: Toss it with your favorite pasta for a classic spaghetti marinara or use it in dishes like lasagna and baked ziti.

2.   Pizza: Spread it on pizza dough as a flavorful pizza sauce, then add your favorite toppings and cheese.

3.   Meatballs: Simmer meatballs in Tomato Marinara Sauce for a delicious meatball marinara sub or as an appetizer.

4.   Eggplant Parmesan: Layer it with breaded and fried eggplant slices and cheese for a comforting Eggplant Parmesan.

5.   Chicken Parmesan: Top breaded and cooked chicken cutlets with marinara sauce and melted cheese for a savory Chicken Parmesan.

Tomato Marinara Sauce is a versatile and essential Italian sauce that can be used in numerous recipes. Its rich tomato flavor and aromatic herbs make it a staple in Italian cuisine, perfect for pasta, pizza, and many other dishes. Enjoy the homemade goodness of Tomato Marinara Sauce in your culinary creations.

Alfredo Sauce Recipe

Ingredients:

·   1/2 cup (1 stick) unsalted butter

·   1 cup heavy cream

·   1 cup grated Parmesan cheese

·   2 cloves garlic, minced

·   Salt and black pepper to taste

·   Optional: Fresh parsley, chopped, for garnish

Instructions:

1.   In a saucepan over medium heat, melt the unsalted butter.

2.   Add the minced garlic to the melted butter and sauté for about 1-2 minutes until it becomes fragrant. Be careful not to let it brown.

3.   Pour in the heavy cream and stir to combine with the butter and garlic. Let it simmer gently for about 2-3 minutes, allowing the mixture to heat through.

4.   Gradually whisk in the grated Parmesan cheese. Continue to whisk until the cheese is fully melted and the sauce becomes smooth and creamy. This should take about 3-5 minutes.

5.   Season the Alfredo Sauce with salt and black pepper to taste. Be mindful of the salt, as Parmesan cheese is naturally salty.

6.   If the sauce is too thick, you can add a splash of milk or more heavy cream to reach your desired consistency.

7.   Remove the sauce from heat.

8.   Serve the Alfredo Sauce immediately over your favorite pasta, such as fettuccine or linguine, or use it in various other dishes.

Suggested Uses for Alfredo Sauce:

1.   Fettuccine Alfredo: Toss the sauce with cooked fettuccine pasta for the classic Fettuccine Alfredo.

2.   Chicken Alfredo: Serve it over grilled or sautéed chicken breasts or chicken cutlets.

3.   Seafood Alfredo: Pair it with seafood like shrimp, scallops, or crab for a luxurious Seafood Alfredo.

4.   Vegetables: Drizzle Alfredo Sauce over steamed or roasted vegetables like broccoli or asparagus.

5.   Pizza: Use it as a creamy pizza sauce or as a drizzle on homemade pizzas.

Alfredo Sauce is a rich and indulgent sauce known for its creamy texture and cheesy flavor. It's a versatile sauce that can elevate pasta dishes and add a touch of decadence to your meals. Enjoy the homemade goodness of Alfredo Sauce in your favorite recipes.

Béchamel Sauce Recipe

Ingredients:

·   2 cups whole milk

·   2 tablespoons unsalted butter

·   2 tablespoons all-purpose flour

·   1/4 teaspoon salt

·   1/8 teaspoon white pepper

·   A pinch of ground nutmeg (optional)

Instructions:

1.   Heat the whole milk in a saucepan over medium heat until it's hot but not boiling. Keep it warm on the stove.

2.   In a separate saucepan, melt the unsalted butter over medium heat.

3.   Add the all-purpose flour to the melted butter and whisk continuously to create a smooth paste. This mixture is called a "roux."

4.   Cook the roux, stirring constantly, for about 2-3 minutes until it turns a light, pale color. Be careful not to let it brown.

5.   Slowly and gradually, begin to add the hot milk to the roux, whisking vigorously to prevent lumps from forming. Continue to add the milk until the mixture is smooth and well combined.

6.   Bring the sauce to a gentle simmer and cook for about 10-15 minutes, stirring frequently, until it thickens and reaches a velvety consistency. The sauce should coat the back of a spoon.

7.   Season the Béchamel Sauce with salt, white pepper, and a pinch of ground nutmeg (if desired). Taste and adjust the seasoning as needed.

8.   Once the Béchamel Sauce is ready, remove it from the heat and use it immediately as a base for other sauces, casseroles, or in various recipes.

Suggested Uses for Béchamel Sauce:

1.   Mornay Sauce: Add grated cheese (such as Gruyère or Parmesan) to Béchamel Sauce to create a Mornay Sauce, perfect for macaroni and cheese or gratin dishes.

2.   Lasagna: Use it as one of the layers in a classic lasagna recipe.

3.   Croque Monsieur/Croque Madame: Use Béchamel Sauce in these deli- cious French sandwiches.

4.   Potato Gratin: Layer it with sliced potatoes and cheese to make a creamy potato gratin.

5.   Creamed Spinach: Combine it with cooked spinach for a classic creamed spinach side dish.

Béchamel Sauce, also known as white sauce, is a fundamental French sauce that serves as the base for many other classic sauces. It's versatile and can be adapted to various recipes and cuisines, making it a valuable addition to any cook's repertoire. Enjoy the creamy and velvety goodness of homemade Béchamel Sauce in your culinary creations.

White Wine Butter Sauce Recipe

Ingredients:

·   1/2 cup dry white wine (e.g., Chardonnay or Sauvignon Blanc)

·   2 tablespoons minced shallots

·   2 cloves garlic, minced

·   1/2 cup heavy cream

·   1/2 cup unsalted butter, cubed

·   Salt and white pepper to taste

·   1 tablespoon fresh lemon juice

·   Fresh parsley, chopped, for garnish (optional)

Instructions:

1.   Add the dry white wine, minced shallots, and minced garlic in a saucepan over medium heat. Bring the mixture to a simmer and cook for about 3-5 minutes or until the wine reduces by half.

2.   Reduce the heat to low and add the heavy cream. Simmer gently for another 3-4 minutes, allowing the mixture to heat through.

3.   Gradually whisk in the cubed unsalted butter, one piece at a time, until each piece is fully melted and the sauce becomes smooth and glossy. Continue to whisk until all the butter is incorporated.

4.   Season the White Wine Butter Sauce with salt and white pepper to taste. Be cautious with the salt, as the butter can already be salty.

5. Stir in the fresh lemon juice to add a bright, citrusy note to the sauce. Taste and adjust the seasoning if needed.

6. Remove the sauce from heat and serve it immediately as a luxurious accompaniment to seafood, poultry, or pasta.

Suggested Uses for White Wine Butter Sauce:

1. Seafood: Drizzle it over grilled or pan-seared fish, shrimp, or scallops.

2. Chicken: Spoon it onto sautéed or grilled chicken breasts or thighs.

3. Pasta: Toss it with cooked pasta, such as linguine or fettuccine, for a delightful pasta dish.

4. Vegetables: Use it as a rich sauce for steamed or roasted vegetables like asparagus or broccoli.

5. Risotto: Add it to your favorite risotto recipe for a creamy and flavorful twist.

White Wine Butter Sauce is a versatile and elegant sauce that adds richness and depth of flavor to a variety of dishes. Its buttery goodness, combined with the subtle notes of white wine and lemon, makes it a favorite among chefs and home cooks alike. Enjoy the homemade luxury of White Wine Butter Sauce in your culinary creations.

Mornay Sauce Recipe

Ingredients:

· 2 tablespoons unsalted butter

· 2 tablespoons all-purpose flour

· 1 1/2 cups whole milk

· 1/2 cup grated Gruyère cheese

· 1/4 cup grated Parmesan cheese

· 1/4 teaspoon salt

· 1/8 teaspoon white pepper

· A pinch of ground nutmeg (optional)

Instructions:

1. In a saucepan, melt the unsalted butter over medium heat.

2. Add the all-purpose flour to the melted butter and whisk continuously to create a smooth paste. This mixture is called a "roux."

3. Cook the roux, stirring constantly, for about 2-3 minutes until it turns a light, pale color. Be careful not to let it brown.

4. Gradually and slowly add the whole milk to the roux, whisking vigorously to prevent lumps from forming. Continue to whisk until the mixture is smooth and well combined.

5.   Cook the sauce over medium heat, stirring frequently, until it thickens and reaches a creamy consistency. This should take about 5-7 minutes.

6.   Stir in the grated Gruyère and Parmesan cheeses, and continue to cook, stirring, until the cheeses are fully melted and the sauce becomes smooth.

7.   Season the Mornay Sauce with salt and white pepper to taste. Add a pinch of ground nutmeg for a hint of warmth if desired.

8.   Remove the sauce from heat and use it immediately as a rich and creamy accompaniment to various dishes.

Suggested Uses for Mornay Sauce:

1.   Macaroni and Cheese: Toss it with cooked macaroni for a decadent macaroni and cheese.

2.   Croque Monsieur/Croque Madame: Use it as a filling or topping for these classic French sandwiches.

3.   Vegetable Gratin: Pour it over steamed or roasted vegetables, like cauliflower or broccoli, and bake until bubbly and golden.

4.   Chicken Divan: Combine it with cooked chicken and broccoli for a Chicken Divan casserole.

5.   Seafood: Serve it as a creamy sauce with seafood, such as poached fish or shrimp.

Mornay Sauce is a cheese-infused béchamel sauce that adds a creamy and indulgent touch to a variety of dishes. Its rich and cheesy flavor makes it a popular choice for comfort food recipes. Enjoy the homemade goodness of Mornay Sauce in your culinary creations.

Dijon Mustard Sauce Recipe

Ingredients:

·   1/2 cup heavy cream

·   2 tablespoons Dijon mustard

·   2 tablespoons unsalted butter

·   1 clove garlic, minced

·   1/4 cup chicken or vegetable broth

·   Salt and black pepper to taste

·   Fresh parsley, chopped, for garnish (optional)

Instructions:

1.   In a saucepan over medium heat, melt the unsalted butter.

2.   Add the minced garlic to the melted butter and sauté for about 1-2 minutes until it becomes fragrant. Be careful not to let

it brown.

3. Pour in the heavy cream and chicken or vegetable broth. Stir to combine.

4. Add the Dijon mustard to the saucepan and whisk until it's fully incorpo- rated into the mixture.

5. Bring the sauce to a gentle simmer and cook for about 3-5 minutes, allowing it to thicken slightly.

6. Season the Dijon Mustard Sauce with salt and black pepper to taste. Adjust the seasoning as needed.

7. Once the sauce has thickened to your desired consistency, remove it from heat.

8. Serve the Dijon Mustard Sauce immediately as a flavorful accompaniment to grilled chicken, pork, or vegetables.

Suggested Uses for Dijon Mustard Sauce:

1. Grilled Chicken: Drizzle it over grilled chicken breasts or thighs for a tangy and creamy chicken dish.

2. Pork Tenderloin: Serve it as a sauce for roasted or grilled pork tenderloin.

3. Vegetables: Use it as a dipping sauce for steamed or roasted vegetables like asparagus or green beans.

4. Sandwiches: Spread it on sandwiches or wraps for added flavor.

5. Seafood: Pair it with grilled or baked fish, such as salmon or trout, for a delicious seafood dish.

Dijon Mustard Sauce is a versatile and tangy condiment that can enhance the flavors of a variety of dishes. Its creamy texture and sharp Dijon mustard flavor make it a delightful addition to meat- and vegetable-based recipes. Enjoy the homemade goodness of Dijon Mustard Sauce in your culinary creations.

Gravy

Onion Gravy Recipe

Ingredients:

- 2 large onions, thinly sliced

- 2 tablespoons unsalted butter

- 2 tablespoons all-purpose flour

- 2 cups beef or vegetable broth

- 1/2 cup red wine (optional)

- Salt and black pepper to taste

- Fresh thyme leaves, chopped, for garnish (optional)

Instructions:

1.   In a large skillet or saucepan, melt the unsalted butter over medium heat.

2.   Add the thinly sliced onions to the melted butter and sauté for about 10-15 minutes, stirring occasionally, until the onions become soft, caramelized, and golden brown.

3.   Sprinkle the all-purpose flour over the caramelized onions and stir well to combine. Cook for an additional 1-2 minutes, allowing the flour to cook and lightly brown.

4.   Gradually add the beef or vegetable broth to the skillet, stirring constantly to prevent lumps from forming. If desired, you can also add the red wine at this stage for extra flavor.

5.   Bring the mixture to a gentle simmer and cook for about 5-7 minutes until the gravy thickens and reaches your desired consistency.

6.   Season the Onion Gravy with salt and black pepper to taste. Adjust the seasoning as needed.

7.   Remove the gravy from heat and serve it immediately as a savory accompaniment to roasted meats, mashed potatoes, or other dishes.

Suggested Uses for Onion Gravy:

1.   Roasted Meats: Serve it with roast beef, chicken, or pork for a classic pairing.

2.   Mashed Potatoes: Pour it over creamy mashed potatoes for a comforting side dish.

3.   Bangers and Mash: Top sausages and mashed potatoes with Onion Gravy for a hearty meal.

4.   Meatloaf: Use it as a flavorful topping for meatloaf.

5.   Yorkshire Puddings: Fill Yorkshire puddings with Onion Gravy for a traditional British treat.

Onion Gravy is a rich and savory sauce with the sweet, caramelized flavor of onions. It's a comforting addition to many dishes, especially those featuring roasted meats and potatoes. Enjoy the homemade goodness of Onion Gravy to elevate your meals.

Mushroom Gravy Recipe

Ingredients:

·   8 ounces mushrooms (button, cremini, or wild mushrooms), finely chopped

·   2 tablespoons unsalted butter

·   2 cloves garlic, minced

·   2 tablespoons all-purpose flour

·   2 cups beef or vegetable broth

·   1/2 cup dry white wine (optional)

·   Salt and black pepper to taste

·   Fresh thyme leaves, chopped, for garnish (optional)

Instructions:

1.   In a large skillet or saucepan, melt the unsalted butter over medium heat.

2.   Add the finely chopped mushrooms to the melted butter and sauté for about 5-7 minutes, stirring occasionally, until they release their moisture and become golden brown.

3.   Stir in the minced garlic and cook for an additional 1-2 minutes until fragrant.

4.   Sprinkle the all-purpose flour over the mushrooms and stir well to combine. Cook for an additional 1-2 minutes, allowing the flour to cook and lightly brown.

5.   Gradually add the beef or vegetable broth to the skillet, stirring constantly to prevent lumps from forming. If desired, you can also add the dry white wine at this stage for extra flavor.

6.   Bring the mixture to a gentle simmer and cook for about 5-7 minutes until the gravy thickens and reaches your desired consistency.

7.   Season the Mushroom Gravy with salt and black pepper to taste. Adjust the seasoning as needed.

8.   Remove the gravy from the heat and serve it immediately as a delicious accompaniment to roasted meats, mashed potatoes, or other dishes.

Suggested Uses for Mushroom Gravy:

1.   Roasted Meats: Serve it alongside roast chicken, turkey, beef, or pork for a savory pairing.

2.   Mashed Potatoes: Drizzle it over creamy mashed potatoes for an earthy, flavorful side dish.

3.   Steak: Pour it over grilled or pan-seared steaks for a delectable sauce.

4.   Meatloaf: Use it as a flavorful topping for meatloaf.

5.   Vegetarian Dishes: Spoon it over vegetarian or vegan dishes for added depth of flavor.

Mushroom Gravy is a hearty and savory sauce that celebrates the earthy richness of mushrooms. It's a versatile condiment that can elevate a variety of dishes, making it a favorite among home cooks and chefs. Enjoy the homemade goodness of Mushroom Gravy in your culinary creations.

Giblet Gravy Recipe

Ingredients:

·   Giblets from a roast turkey or chicken (heart, liver, gizzard, and neck)

·   1 small onion, finely chopped

·   1 small carrot, finely chopped

·   1 celery stalk, finely chopped

·   2 cups chicken or turkey broth

- 2 tablespoons all-purpose flour

- 2 tablespoons unsalted butter

- Salt and black pepper to taste

Instructions:

1.   Rinse the giblets under cold water and remove any excess fat or impurities. Set them aside.

2.   In a saucepan, melt the unsalted butter over medium heat.

3.   Add the chopped onion, carrot, and celery to the melted butter. Sauté the vegetables for about 5-7 minutes until they become tender and slightly golden.

4.   Add the giblets (heart, liver, gizzard, and neck) to the sautéed vegetables. Cook for another 5-7 minutes, stirring occasionally, until the giblets are browned.

5.   Sprinkle the all-purpose flour over the giblets and vegetables. Stir well to combine and cook for an additional 1-2 minutes to remove the raw flour taste.

6.   Gradually add the chicken or turkey broth to the saucepan, stirring constantly to prevent lumps. Bring the mixture to a gentle simmer.

7.   Reduce the heat to low, cover the saucepan, and let it simmer for about 30-45 minutes. This allows the giblets to become tender and infuse the broth with flavor. Stir occasionally.

8.   After simmering, remove the giblets from the broth and set them aside. If desired, you can chop them finely and add them back into the gravy.

9.   Strain the broth through a fine-mesh sieve or cheesecloth into a clean saucepan, discarding the cooked vegetables.

10.   Bring the strained broth back to a simmer. If you've chopped the giblets, you can add them back into the gravy at this point.

11.   Continue simmering for about 10-15 minutes until the gravy thickens to your desired consistency. If it's too thick, you can add a bit more broth to adjust.

12.   Season the Giblet Gravy with salt and black pepper to taste. Adjust the seasoning as needed.

13.   Serve the Giblet Gravy hot as a flavorful accompaniment to roast turkey, chicken, or other poultry dishes.

Suggested Uses for Giblet Gravy:

1.   Roast Turkey: Serve it alongside roast turkey for a classic Thanksgiving pairing.

2.   Roast Chicken: Use it as a delicious topping for roast chicken.

3.   Mashed Potatoes: Drizzle it over creamy mashed potatoes for added richness.

4.   Stuffing: Pour it over your favorite stuffing or dressing.

5.   Biscuits: Serve it with biscuits for a comforting breakfast or brunch.

Giblet Gravy is a traditional and flavorful sauce that complements poultry dishes wonderfully. It's a classic addition to holiday feasts and special occasions. Enjoy the homemade goodness of Giblet Gravy in your culinary creations.

Red Wine Gravy Recipe

Ingredients:

- 1 cup red wine (dry red wine such as Cabernet Sauvignon or Merlot)
- 2 cups beef or vegetable broth
- 2 tablespoons unsalted butter
- 2 tablespoons all-purpose flour
- 1 small onion, finely chopped
- 2 cloves garlic, minced
- 1 sprig fresh thyme (or 1/2 teaspoon dried thyme)
- Salt and black pepper to taste

Instructions:

1. In a saucepan over medium heat, melt the unsalted butter.

2. Add the finely chopped onion to the melted butter and sauté for about 5 minutes until it becomes soft and translucent.

3. Stir in the minced garlic and cook for an additional 1-2 minutes until fragrant.

4. Sprinkle the all-purpose flour over the sautéed onions and garlic. Stir well to create a smooth paste (roux) and cook for about 1-2 minutes, allowing the roux to lightly brown.

5. Gradually add the red wine to the roux, whisking constantly to prevent lumps from forming. Continue to whisk until the mixture is smooth and well combined.

6. Add the beef or vegetable broth and the sprig of fresh thyme (or dried thyme) to the saucepan. Stir to combine.

7. Bring the mixture to a gentle simmer and cook for about 10-15 minutes, or until the gravy thickens to your desired consistency. Stir occasionally.

8. Season the Red Wine Gravy with salt and black pepper to taste. Remove the sprig of fresh thyme, if used, before serving. Adjust the seasoning as needed.

9. Serve the Red Wine Gravy hot as a rich and savory accompaniment to roast beef, lamb, or other dishes.

Suggested Uses for Red Wine Gravy:

1. Roast Beef: Pair it with roast beef for a classic and luxurious combination.

2. Roast Lamb: Serve it alongside roast lamb for a delightful flavor pairing.

3. Steak: Drizzle it over grilled or pan-seared steaks for an elegant sauce.

4. Mashed Potatoes: Pour it over creamy mashed potatoes for a gourmet side dish.

5. Meatballs: Use it as a sauce for meatballs or meatloaf for added depth of flavor.

Red Wine Gravy is a sumptuous and sophisticated sauce that elevates the flavor of meat dishes, especially roasts. Its rich and velvety texture, combined with the boldness of red wine, makes it a favorite among connoisseurs. Enjoy the homemade goodness of Red Wine Gravy in your culinary creations.

Au Jus Gravy Recipe

Ingredients:

·   Drippings from a roast (beef, pork, or lamb)

·   2 cups beef broth (or chicken broth for pork or lamb)

·   1/2 cup dry red wine (optional)

·   2 cloves garlic, minced

·   Salt and black pepper to taste

Instructions:

1.   After roasting your meat, remove it from the roasting pan and transfer it to a serving platter. Cover it loosely with foil to keep it warm.

2.   Place the roasting pan with the drippings on the stovetop over medium heat.

3.   Add minced garlic to the drippings and sauté for about 1-2 minutes until fragrant.

4.   If using, pour in the dry red wine and stir, scraping the browned bits from the bottom of the pan. Allow the wine to simmer and reduce slightly, about 3-5 minutes.

5.   Pour in the beef broth (or chicken broth for pork or lamb) and stir to combine with the drippings.

6.   Bring the mixture to a gentle simmer and cook for about 5-7 minutes, allowing the flavors to meld.

7.   Taste the Au Jus Gravy and season with salt and black pepper as needed. Adjust the seasoning to your preference.

8.   Once the gravy is heated through and well-seasoned, remove it from heat.

9.   Strain the Au Jus Gravy through a fine-mesh sieve or cheesecloth into a serving container to remove any solids, leaving you with a smooth and flavorful sauce.

10.   Serve the Au Jus Gravy hot alongside your roasted meat for a simple and delicious enhancement.

Suggested Uses for Au Jus Gravy:

1.   Prime Rib: Serve it with prime rib for a classic pairing.

2.   Roast Beef: Drizzle it over slices of roast beef for added juiciness and flavor.

3.   Pork Roast: Pair it with roasted pork loin or pork shoulder.

4.   Lamb: Use it as a dipping sauce for roast lamb.

Au Jus Gravy is a natural and savory sauce that enhances the flavors of roasted meats. It's a simple yet delicious way to enjoy the juices and drippings from your roast. Enjoy the homemade goodness of Au Jus Gravy in your culinary creations.

Vegetarian Gravy Recipe

Ingredients:

- 2 tablespoons unsalted butter or vegetable oil
- 1 small onion, finely chopped
- 2 cloves garlic, minced
- 2 tablespoons all-purpose flour
- 2 cups vegetable broth
- 1/2 cup dry white wine (optional)
- 1 teaspoon soy sauce or tamari (for umami flavor)
- Salt and black pepper to taste
- Fresh thyme leaves, chopped, for garnish (optional)

Instructions:

1. In a saucepan over medium heat, melt the unsalted butter or heat the vegetable oil.

2. Add the finely chopped onion to the melted butter or heated oil. Sauté for about 5 minutes until the onion becomes soft and translucent.

3. Stir in the minced garlic and cook for an additional 1-2 minutes until fragrant.

4. Sprinkle the all-purpose flour over the sautéed onion and garlic. Stir well to create a smooth paste (roux) and cook for about 1-2 minutes, allowing the roux to lightly brown.

5. Gradually add the vegetable broth to the saucepan, stirring constantly to prevent lumps from forming. Continue to whisk until the mixture is smooth and well combined.

6. If using, pour in the dry white wine and stir. Allow the wine to simmer and reduce slightly, about 3-5 minutes.

7. Add the soy sauce or tamari to the gravy for umami flavor. Stir to incorporate.

8. Bring the mixture to a gentle simmer and cook for about 10-15 minutes, or until the gravy thickens to your desired consistency. Stir occasionally.

9. Season the Vegetarian Gravy with salt and black pepper to taste. Adjust the seasoning as needed.

10. Remove the gravy from heat and serve it hot as a flavorful accompaniment to mashed potatoes, roasted vegetables, or other vegetarian dishes.

Suggested Uses for Vegetarian Gravy:

1.   Mashed Potatoes: Drizzle it over creamy mashed potatoes for a comfort- ing side dish.

2.   Roasted Vegetables: Pour it over a medley of roasted vegetables for added richness.

3.   Vegetarian Roasts: Serve it with vegetarian roasts or nut roasts for a hearty meal.

4.   Pasta: Use it as a sauce for pasta dishes, like pappardelle or mushroom pasta.

5.   Meatless Loaf: Spoon it over vegetarian meatloaf for extra flavor.

Vegetarian Gravy is a delicious and meat-free alternative to traditional gravy. It's perfect for vegetarian and vegan meals, adding depth and richness to a variety of dishes. Enjoy the homemade goodness of Vegetarian Gravy in your culinary creations.

Country Gravy Recipe

Ingredients:

·   1/4 cup unsalted butter

·   1/4 cup all-purpose flour

·   2 cups whole milk

·   Salt and black pepper to taste

Instructions:

1.   In a skillet or saucepan over medium heat, melt the unsalted butter.

2.   Once the butter is melted and bubbling, sprinkle the all-purpose flour evenly over it. Whisk constantly to combine the flour and butter. Continue to cook and whisk for about 1-2 minutes, or until the mixture (roux) becomes a light golden color. Be careful not to let it brown too much.

3.   Gradually add the whole milk to the roux, pouring it in a little at a time while whisking vigorously to prevent lumps. Continue to whisk until the mixture is smooth and well combined.

4.   Reduce the heat to low and let the gravy simmer gently for about 5-7 minutes, stirring frequently, until it thickens to your desired consistency.

5.   Season the Country Gravy with salt and black pepper to taste. Adjust the seasoning as needed.

6.   Remove the gravy from heat and serve it hot as a comforting accompani- ment to biscuits, fried chicken, chicken-fried steak, or other Southern dishes.

Suggested Uses for Country Gravy:

1.   Biscuits and Gravy: Pour it generously over freshly baked biscuits for the classic Southern breakfast dish.

2.   Fried Chicken: Serve it as a topping for crispy fried chicken, creating a delicious combination known as chicken and gravy.

3.   Chicken-Fried Steak: Use it as a creamy sauce for chicken-fried steak, a Southern favorite.

4.   Mashed Potatoes: Drizzle it over creamy mashed potatoes for added flavor.

5.   Sausage Patties: Pair it with sausage patties for a hearty breakfast.

Country Gravy is a Southern staple that adds creamy and savory goodness to a variety of dishes. Whether you're enjoying it for breakfast or as a comforting dinner, this classic gravy is sure to satisfy your cravings. Enjoy the homemade goodness of Country Gravy in your Southern-inspired meals.

Sausage Gravy Recipe

Ingredients:

·   1 pound (16 oz) ground pork sausage (mild or hot, as preferred)

·   1/4 cup all-purpose flour

·   2 cups whole milk

·   Salt and black pepper to taste

·   Optional: Dash of cayenne pepper for a slight kick (adjust to taste)

Instructions:

1.   In a large skillet or frying pan, cook 1 pound of ground pork sausage over medium-high heat, breaking it apart with a spatula as it cooks. Cook until the sausage is browned and fully cooked, usually about 8-10 minutes.

2.   Reduce the heat to medium-low and sprinkle 1/4 cup of all-purpose flour over the cooked sausage. Stir well to combine, ensuring that the flour is evenly distributed and coats the sausage. Continue to cook for an additional 2-3 minutes, allowing the flour to cook slightly.

3.   Gradually pour in 2 cups of whole milk while stirring continuously to prevent lumps from forming. Keep stirring until the mixture thickens and reaches your desired consistency, typically about 5-7 minutes.

4.   Season the sausage gravy with salt, black pepper, and, if desired, a dash of cayenne pepper for some heat. Adjust the seasoning to taste.

5.   Continue to cook for another minute or two, stirring constantly, until the gravy is smooth and thickened.

6.   Remove the skillet from heat and let the sausage gravy sit for a couple of minutes to thicken further before serving.

Suggested Uses for Sausage Gravy:

1.   Biscuits and Gravy: Serve the sausage gravy over freshly baked biscuits for the classic Southern dish known as "Biscuits and Gravy."

2.   Breakfast Burrito Filling: Use the sausage gravy as a filling for breakfast burritos, scrambled eggs, and cheese.

3.   Country Fried Steak Topping: Pour the sausage gravy over country-fried steak for a hearty and indulgent meal.

4.   Mashed Potato Accompaniment: Spoon the gravy over mashed potatoes for a flavorful side dish.

5.   Savory Crepe Filling: Fill savory crepes with sausage gravy and sautéed vegetables for a delicious brunch option.

Enjoy your homemade Sausage Gravy in various ways, from breakfast classics to hearty dinner options!

Rosemary Gravy Recipe

Ingredients:

·   2 tablespoons unsalted butter

·   2 tablespoons all-purpose flour

·   2 cups chicken or turkey broth

·   1 sprig fresh rosemary (or 1/2 teaspoon dried rosemary)

·   Salt and black pepper to taste

Instructions:

1.   In a saucepan over medium heat, melt the unsalted butter.

2.   Once the butter is melted and bubbling, sprinkle the all-purpose flour evenly over it. Whisk constantly to combine the flour and butter. Continue to cook and whisk for about 1-2 minutes, or until the mixture (roux) becomes a light golden color. Be careful not to let it brown too much.

3.   Gradually add the chicken or turkey broth to the roux, pouring it in a little at a time while whisking vigorously to prevent lumps. Continue to whisk until the mixture is smooth and well combined.

4.   Add the fresh rosemary sprig (or dried rosemary) to the gravy. Stir to incorporate.

5.   Bring the mixture to a gentle simmer and cook for about 5-7 minutes, allowing the rosemary to infuse its flavor into the gravy and until it thickens to your desired consistency. Stir occasionally.

6.   Season the Rosemary Gravy with salt and black pepper to taste. Adjust the seasoning as needed.

7.   Remove the gravy from heat and serve it hot as a fragrant and savory accompaniment to roast chicken, turkey, or other dishes.

Suggested Uses for Rosemary Gravy:

1.   Roast Chicken: Drizzle it over roast chicken for a delightful flavor pairing.

2.   Roast Turkey: Serve it alongside roast turkey for a classic and aromatic combination.

3.   Mashed Potatoes: Pour it over creamy mashed potatoes for added richness and a hint of rosemary flavor.

4.   Pork Roast: Use it as a sauce for roast pork loin or tenderloin.

5.   Vegetarian Dishes: Spoon it over vegetarian or vegan dishes for a rosemary-infused twist.

Rosemary Gravy is a fragrant and herb-infused sauce that enhances the flavors of roast poultry and other dishes. Its aromatic profile adds depth and character to your meals. Enjoy the homemade goodness of Rosemary Gravy in your culinary creations

Sage Gravy Recipe

Ingredients:

·   2 tablespoons unsalted butter

·   2 tablespoons all-purpose flour

·   2 cups chicken or turkey broth

·   4-6 fresh sage leaves (or 1 teaspoon dried sage)

·   Salt and black pepper to taste

Instructions:

1.   In a saucepan over medium heat, melt the unsalted butter.

2.   Once the butter is melted and bubbling, sprinkle the all-purpose flour evenly over it. Whisk constantly to combine the flour and butter. Continue to cook and whisk for about 1-2 minutes, or until the mixture (roux) becomes a light golden color. Be careful not to let it brown too much.

3.   Gradually add the chicken or turkey broth to the roux, pouring it in a little at a time while whisking vigorously to prevent lumps. Continue to whisk until the mixture is smooth and well combined.

4.   Add the fresh sage leaves (or dried sage) to the gravy. Stir to incorporate.

5.   Bring the mixture to a gentle simmer and cook for about 5-7 minutes, allowing the sage to infuse its flavor into the gravy and until it thickens to your desired consistency. Stir occasionally.

6.   Season the Sage Gravy with salt and black pepper to taste. Adjust the seasoning as needed.

7.   Remove the gravy from heat, and if using fresh sage leaves, remove them from the gravy.

8.   Serve the Sage Gravy hot as a fragrant and savory accompaniment to roast chicken, turkey, or other dishes.

Suggested Uses for Sage Gravy:

1.   Roast Chicken: Drizzle it over roast chicken for a delightful flavor pairing.

2.   Roast Turkey: Serve it alongside roast turkey for a classic and aromatic combination.

3.   Mashed Potatoes: Pour it over creamy mashed potatoes for added richness and a hint of sage flavor.

4.   Pork Roast: Use it as a sauce for roast pork loin or tenderloin.

5.   Vegetarian Dishes: Spoon it over vegetarian or vegan dishes for a sage- infused twist.

Sage Gravy is a flavorful and herb-infused sauce that enhances the flavors of roast poultry and other dishes. Its aromatic profile adds depth and character to your meals. Enjoy the homemade goodness of Sage Gravy in your culinary creations.

Salsas

Pico de Gallo Recipe

Ingredients:

- 4 medium ripe tomatoes, diced

- 1 small red onion, finely chopped

- 1/2 cup fresh cilantro, chopped

- 1-2 jalapeño peppers, finely chopped (adjust to taste)

- 2-3 cloves garlic, minced

- Juice of 1-2 limes, to taste

- 1/2 teaspoon kosher salt, or to taste

- 1/4 teaspoon black pepper, or to taste

Instructions:

1.   In a mixing bowl, combine the diced ripe tomatoes, finely chopped red onion, chopped fresh cilantro, finely chopped jalapeño peppers (adjust the quantity to your preferred level of spiciness), and minced garlic.

2.   Squeeze the juice of 1-2 limes over the mixture. Start with one lime and add more to taste if desired.

3.   Season the Pico de Gallo with kosher salt and black pepper.

4.   Gently toss all the ingredients together until they are well combined.

5.   Taste the Pico de Gallo and adjust the spiciness, acidity, or seasoning level by adding more jalapeño, lime juice, salt, or pepper as needed.

6.   Let the Pico de Gallo sit at room temperature for about 15-30 minutes before serving to allow the flavors to meld together. You can also refrigerate it for later use.

Suggested Uses for Pico de Gallo:

1.   Taco Topping: Serve Pico de Gallo as a fresh and zesty topping for tacos, whether they are filled with grilled chicken, beef, shrimp, or vegetables.

2.   Tortilla Chip Dip: Use it as a flavorful dip for tortilla chips or corn chips.

3.   Salsa for Grilled Meats: Pair Pico de Gallo with grilled meats like steak or chicken for a burst of freshness and flavor.

4.   Burrito or Quesadilla Filling: Include it as a filling for burritos or quesadillas to add a refreshing contrast to the melted cheese and protein.

5.   Salad Enhancer: Sprinkle it on top of a salad to elevate the taste and add a Mexican twist to your greens.

Pico de Gallo is a classic Mexican salsa made with fresh ingredients like tomatoes, onions, cilantro, and jalapeños. It's known for its vibrant flavors and versatility, making it an excellent addition to various dishes and a must-have condiment for Mexican cuisine lovers. Enjoy experimenting with different recipes to showcase the deliciousness of this simple and refreshing Pico de Gallo.

Mango Salsa Recipe

Ingredients:

·   2 ripe mangoes, peeled, pitted, and diced

·   1/2 red onion, finely chopped

·   1 red bell pepper, finely chopped

·   1/2 cup fresh cilantro, chopped

·   1-2 jalapeño peppers, finely chopped (adjust to taste)

·   Juice of 2 limes

·   1 teaspoon honey (optional)

·   1/2 teaspoon kosher salt, or to taste

·   1/4 teaspoon black pepper, or to taste

Instructions:

1.   In a mixing bowl, combine the diced ripe mangoes, finely chopped red onion, finely chopped red bell pepper, chopped fresh cilantro, and finely chopped jalapeño peppers (adjust the quantity to your preferred level of spiciness).

2.   Squeeze the juice of 2 limes over the mixture.

3.   If you prefer a slightly sweeter salsa, add 1 teaspoon of honey (optional).

4.   Season the Mango Salsa with kosher salt and black pepper.

5.   Gently toss all the ingredients together until they are well combined.

6.   Taste the Mango Salsa and adjust the sweetness, spiciness, acidity, or seasoning level by adding more honey, jalapeño, lime juice, salt, or pepper as needed.

7.   Let the Mango Salsa sit at room temperature for about 15-30 minutes before serving to allow the flavors to meld together. You can also refrigerate it for later use.

Suggested Uses for Mango Salsa:

1.   Grilled Chicken Topping: Serve Mango Salsa as a fruity and tangy topping for grilled chicken breasts or thighs.

2.   Fish or Seafood Salsa: Pair it with grilled or pan-seared fish or seafood, such as salmon or shrimp, for a tropical flavor combination.

3.   Taco Filling: Use Mango Salsa as a filling for soft tacos or fish tacos to add a refreshing twist.

4.   Salsa for Pork: Enjoy it as a salsa for grilled or roasted pork, like pork chops or tenderloin.

5.   Chips and Dip: Serve Mango Salsa as a flavorful dip for tortilla chips, pita chips, or even as a side for nachos.

Mango Salsa is a delightful and refreshing salsa that combines the sweetness of ripe mangoes with the zing of lime juice and the vibrant colors and flavors of red onion, red bell pepper, and cilantro. It's a versatile condiment that adds a tropical touch to your dishes and works wonderfully as a topping or side. Enjoy experimenting with different recipes to showcase the deliciousness of this fruity and tangy Mango Salsa.

Pineapple Salsa Recipe

Ingredients:

- ·   2 cups fresh pineapple, diced
- ·   1/2 red onion, finely chopped
- ·   1 red bell pepper, finely chopped
- ·   1/2 cup fresh cilantro, chopped
- ·   1-2 jalapeño peppers, finely chopped (adjust to taste)
- ·   Juice of 2 limes
- ·   1 teaspoon honey (optional)
- ·   1/2 teaspoon kosher salt, or to taste
- ·   1/4 teaspoon black pepper, or to taste

Instructions:

1.   In a mixing bowl, combine the diced fresh pineapple, finely chopped red onion, finely chopped red bell pepper, cho-

pped fresh cilantro, and finely chopped jalapeño peppers (adjust the quantity to your preferred level of spiciness).

2.   Squeeze the juice of 2 limes over the mixture.

3.   If you prefer a slightly sweeter salsa, add 1 teaspoon of honey (optional).

4.   Season the Pineapple Salsa with kosher salt and black pepper.

5.   Gently toss all the ingredients together until they are well combined.

6.   Taste the Pineapple Salsa and adjust the level of sweetness, spiciness, acidity, or seasoning by adding more honey, jalapeño, lime juice, salt, or pepper as needed.

7.   Let the Pineapple Salsa sit at room temperature for about 15-30 minutes before serving to allow the flavors to meld together. You can also refrigerate it for later use.

Suggested Uses for Pineapple Salsa:

1.   Grilled Chicken Topping: Serve Pineapple Salsa as a sweet and tangy topping for grilled chicken, adding a tropical flair to your dish.

2.   Fish or Seafood Salsa: Pair it with grilled or pan-seared fish or seafood, such as mahi-mahi or shrimp, for a delightful flavor combination.

3.   Pork Salsa: Enjoy it as a salsa for grilled or roasted pork, like pork tenderloin or pork chops, for a hint of sweetness.

4.   Tropical Tacos: Use Pineapple Salsa as a filling for tacos, especially with

grilled or blackened chicken or fish.

5.   Chips and Dip: Serve Pineapple Salsa as a refreshing dip for tortilla chips, pita chips, or as a side for nachos.

Pineapple Salsa is a tropical and refreshing salsa that combines the natural sweetness of fresh pineapple with the zesty kick of jalapeño peppers and the vibrant colors and flavors of red onion, red bell pepper, and cilantro. It's a versatile condiment that adds a burst of flavor to your dishes and brings a taste of the tropics to your table. Enjoy experimenting with different recipes to showcase the deliciousness of this fruity and tangy Pineapple Salsa.

Roasted Tomato Salsa Recipe

Ingredients:

·   4 ripe tomatoes

·   1/2 red onion, roughly chopped

·   2 cloves garlic, peeled

·   2 jalapeño peppers

- 1/4 cup fresh cilantro, chopped

- Juice of 1 lime

- 1/2 teaspoon kosher salt, or to taste

- 1/4 teaspoon black pepper, or to taste

- 1/4 teaspoon cumin (optional, for added depth of flavor)

Instructions:

1. Preheat your broiler or grill to high heat.

2. Place the ripe tomatoes, red onion, garlic cloves, and jalapeño peppers on a baking sheet or grill grates.

3. Roast or grill the vegetables until they are charred and blistered, turning them occasionally to ensure even cooking. This will take about 10-15 minutes.

4. Remove the roasted vegetables from the heat source and let them cool slightly.

5. Once the vegetables are cool enough to handle, peel the skin off the tomatoes and remove the stems from the jalapeño peppers. You can also remove the seeds from the jalapeño peppers if you prefer a milder salsa.

6. Place the roasted tomatoes, red onion, garlic cloves, jalapeño peppers, chopped fresh cilantro, and juice of 1 lime in a blender or food processor.

7. Pulse the mixture until it reaches your desired salsa consistency. You can make it chunky or smooth, depending on your preference.

8. Season the Roasted Tomato Salsa with kosher salt, black pepper, and cumin (if using). Blend or pulse again to incorporate the seasonings.

9. Taste the salsa and adjust the spiciness, acidity, or seasoning level by adding more jalapeño, lime juice, salt, or pepper as needed.

10. Transfer the Roasted Tomato Salsa to a serving bowl or container. You can serve it immediately or refrigerate it for later use.

Suggested Uses for Roasted Tomato Salsa:

1. Chips and Dip: Serve it as a classic dip for tortilla chips or alongside other appetizers.

2. Taco Topping: Use Roasted Tomato Salsa as a flavorful topping for tacos filled with your favorite ingredients.

3. Enchilada Sauce: Pour it over enchiladas before baking for added flavor and moisture.

4. Grilled Meats: Serve it as a condiment for grilled meats like steak, chicken, or pork.

5. Eggs: Top scrambled eggs or omelets with a spoonful of Roasted Tomato Salsa for a delicious breakfast.

Roasted Tomato Salsa offers a smoky and charred flavor that comes from roasting the tomatoes, onions, and jalapeño peppers. It's a versatile salsa that adds depth and complexity to your dishes, making it a flavorful addition to your culinary repertoire. Enjoy experimenting with different recipes to showcase the deliciousness of this roasted tomato salsa.

Roasted Red Pepper Salsa Recipe

Ingredients:

- 2 large red bell peppers
- 1 small red onion, finely chopped
- 2 cloves garlic, minced
- 2 tablespoons fresh cilantro, chopped
- 1 tablespoon fresh lime juice
- 1 tablespoon olive oil
- 1/2 teaspoon ground cumin
- Salt and black pepper to taste

Instructions:

1. Preheat your oven's broiler to high.

2. Place the red bell peppers on a baking sheet lined with aluminum foil. Broil the peppers, turning occasionally, until the skin is charred and blistered on all sides. This will take about 10-15 minutes.

3. Remove the peppers from the oven and immediately transfer them to a bowl. Cover the bowl with plastic wrap or a kitchen towel and let the peppers steam for about 10 minutes. This will make it easier to peel off the skin.

4. Once the peppers have steamed, peel off the charred skin, remove the seeds and stems, and finely chop the roasted red peppers.

5. Combine the roasted red peppers, finely chopped red onion, minced garlic, chopped cilantro, fresh lime juice, olive oil, and ground cumin in a mixing bowl. Mix well to combine all the ingredients.

6. Season the salsa with salt and black pepper to taste. Adjust the seasoning to your preference.

7. Cover the Roasted Red Pepper Salsa and refrigerate it for at least 30 minutes to allow the flavors to meld and develop.

8. Serve the salsa chilled with tortilla chips or as a versatile accompaniment to a variety of dishes.

Suggested Uses for Roasted Red Pepper Salsa:

1. Tortilla Chips: Enjoy it as a delicious dip with crispy tortilla chips for a classic snack or appetizer.

2. Grilled Chicken: Spoon it over grilled chicken breasts or thighs for a burst of flavor and color.

3. Fish Tacos: Use it as a topping for fish tacos, enhancing their taste with a zesty kick.

4. Bruschetta: Spread it on toasted baguette slices for a vibrant and flavorful bruschetta.

5. Salad Dressing: Mix it into your favorite salad dressing to add a tangy twist to your salads.

This Roasted Red Pepper Salsa is a versatile and vibrant addition to your culinary repertoire. Its smoky, sweet, and slightly tangy flavors make it a delightful complement to a wide range of dishes. Enjoy the homemade goodness of this salsa in your cooking adventures.

Avocado Salsa Recipe

Ingredients:

·   4 tomatillos, husked and rinsed

·   1 small onion, roughly chopped

·   2 jalapeño peppers, stemmed and seeds removed for milder heat

·   2 ripe avocados, peeled, pitted, and diced

·   2 cloves garlic, minced

·   2 tablespoons fresh cilantro, chopped

·   2 tablespoons fresh lime juice

·   Salt and black pepper to taste

Instructions:

1.   In a saucepan, bring water to a boil. Add the tomatillos, onion, and jalapeño peppers. Boil for about 10-15 minutes, or until they are soft and slightly tender.

2.   Drain the boiled tomatillos, onion, and jalapeños, and let them cool for a few minutes.

3.   Transfer the boiled ingredients to a food processor.

4.   Add the diced avocados, minced garlic, chopped cilantro, and fresh lime juice to the food processor with the boiled ingredients.

5.   Blend the mixture until it reaches your desired consistency. Depending on your preference, you can make it smooth or leave it slightly chunky.

6.   Season the Creamy Avocado Salsa with salt and black pepper to taste. Adjust the seasoning to your liking.

7.   Transfer the salsa to a serving bowl.

8.   Chill the salsa in the refrigerator for at least 30 minutes to allow the flavors to meld.

9.   Serve the Creamy Avocado Salsa as a delightful dip for tortilla chips or as a versatile topping for various dishes.

Suggested Uses for Avocado Salsa:

1.   Taco Topping: Serve Avocado Salsa as a creamy and tangy topping for tacos, whether they are filled with grilled chicken, beef, shrimp, or vegetables.

2.   Nachos: Use it as a flavorful and refreshing topping for nachos, along with melted cheese and other toppings of your choice.

3.　　　Burrito Filling: Include it as a filling for burritos to add a creamy and zesty contrast to the ingredients.

4.　　　Grilled Meats: Serve it as a condiment for grilled meats like steak, chicken, or fish.

5.　　　Salad Enhancer: Spoon it on top of a salad to give it a rich and creamy avocado flavor.

Avocado Salsa is a creamy and tangy salsa that combines the creaminess of ripe avocados with the zing of lime juice and the vibrant colors and flavors of tomato, red onion, jalapeño pepper, and cilantro. It's a versatile condiment that adds a burst of flavor and creaminess to your dishes, making it a flavorful addition to your culinary repertoire. Enjoy experimenting with different recipes to showcase the deliciousness of this avocado salsa.

Corn and Black Bean Salsa Recipe

Ingredients:

- 1 can (15 ounces) black beans, drained and rinsed

- 1 cup corn kernels (fresh, frozen, or canned)

- 1 red bell pepper, finely chopped

- 1/2 red onion, finely chopped

- 1/2 cup fresh cilantro, chopped

- Juice of 2 limes

- 1-2 jalapeño peppers, finely chopped (adjust to taste)

- 2 cloves garlic, minced

- 1/2 teaspoon ground cumin

- 1/2 teaspoon chili powder (adjust to taste)

- 1/2 teaspoon kosher salt, or to taste

- 1/4 teaspoon black pepper, or to taste

Instructions:

1.　　　Combine the drained and rinsed black beans, corn kernels, finely chopped red bell pepper, finely chopped red onion, and chopped fresh cilantro in a large mixing bowl.

2.　　　Squeeze the juice of 2 limes over the mixture.

3.　　　Add the finely chopped jalapeño peppers (adjust the quantity to your preferred level of spiciness) and minced garlic to the bowl.

4.　　　Season the Corn and Black Bean Salsa with ground cumin, chili powder (adjust to your preferred level of spiciness), kosher salt, and black pepper.

5.　　　Gently toss all the ingredients together until they are well combined.

6. Taste the salsa and adjust the level of spiciness, acidity, or seasoning by adding more jalapeño, lime juice, chili powder, salt, or pepper as needed.

7. Let the Corn and Black Bean Salsa sit at room temperature for about 15-30 minutes before serving to allow the flavors to meld together. You can also refrigerate it for later use.

Suggested Uses for Corn and Black Bean Salsa:

1. Tortilla Chip Dip: Serve it as a delicious dip for tortilla chips, corn chips, or pita chips.

2. Taco Topping: Use it as a flavorful topping for tacos filled with grilled chicken, beef, shrimp, or vegetables.

3. Burrito Filling: Include it as a filling for burritos to add a hearty and satisfying element.

4. Grilled Meat Garnish: Spoon it over grilled meats like steak, chicken, or pork for added flavor and texture.

5. Side Salad: Serve it as a side salad for a barbecue or picnic, or enjoy it as a light and healthy snack.

Corn and Black Bean Salsa is a hearty and flavorful salsa that combines the sweetness of corn with the earthiness of black beans and the zing of lime juice and spices. It's a versatile condiment that adds a satisfying and vibrant touch to your dishes, making it a flavorful addition to your culinary repertoire. Enjoy experimenting with different recipes to showcase the deliciousness of this corn and black bean salsa.

Tomatillo Salsa Recipe

Ingredients:

· 6-8 tomatillos, husked and rinsed

· 2-3 cloves garlic, peeled

· 1/2 white onion, roughly chopped

· 1-2 jalapeño peppers, stems removed (adjust to taste)

· 1/2 cup fresh cilantro, chopped

· Juice of 2 limes

· 1/2 teaspoon kosher salt, or to taste

· 1/4 teaspoon black pepper, or to taste

Instructions:

1. Place the tomatillos, garlic cloves, roughly chopped white onion, and jalapeño peppers on a baking sheet.

2. Roast the vegetables under a broiler or on a grill until they are charred and blistered, turning them occasionally to ensure even cooking. This will take about 10-15 minutes.

3. Remove the roasted vegetables from the heat source and let them cool slightly.

4.   Once the vegetables are cool enough to handle, transfer them to a blender or food processor.

5.   Add the chopped fresh cilantro and squeeze the juice of 2 limes into the blender or food processor.

6.   Season the Tomatillo Salsa with kosher salt and black pepper.

7.   Blend the mixture until it reaches your desired salsa consistency. You can make it chunky or smooth, depending on your preference.

8.   Taste the salsa and adjust the spiciness, acidity, or seasoning level by adding more jalapeño, lime juice, salt, or pepper as needed.

9.   Transfer the Tomatillo Salsa to a serving bowl or container. You can serve it immediately or refrigerate it for later use.

Suggested Uses for Tomatillo Salsa:

1.   Tortilla Chip Dip: Serve it as a zesty dip for tortilla, corn, or pita chips.

2.   Enchilada Sauce: Use it as a flavorful sauce for enchiladas before baking for added depth of flavor.

3.   Taco Topping: Spoon it over tacos filled with grilled chicken, beef, shrimp, or vegetables.

4.   Grilled Meats: Serve it as a condiment for grilled meats like steak, pork, or chicken.

5.   Breakfast Burrito Filling: Include it as a filling for breakfast burritos to add a tangy kick to your morning meal.

Tomatillo Salsa, also known as Salsa Verde, is a tangy and zesty salsa made from roasted tomatillos, garlic, and jalapeño peppers. It's known for its bright green color and versatile use in Mexican cuisine. This salsa adds a delightful tanginess and heat to your dishes and can be enjoyed in a variety of ways. Enjoy experimenting with different recipes to showcase the deliciousness of this Tomatillo Salsa.

Watermelon Salsa Recipe

Ingredients:

·   2 cups diced watermelon (seedless)

·   1/2 cucumber, peeled and diced

·   1/2 red onion, finely chopped

·   1 jalapeño pepper, finely chopped (adjust to taste)

·   1/4 cup fresh mint leaves, chopped

·   Juice of 2 limes

·   1 tablespoon honey (optional, for added sweetness)

·   1/2 teaspoon kosher salt, or to taste

·   1/4 teaspoon black pepper, or to taste

Instructions:

1.   In a mixing bowl, combine the diced watermelon, peeled and diced cucumber, finely chopped red onion, finely chopped jalapeño pepper (adjust the quantity to your preferred level of spiciness), and chopped fresh mint leaves.

2.   Squeeze the juice of 2 limes over the mixture.

3.   If you prefer a slightly sweeter salsa, add 1 tablespoon of honey (adjust to taste).

4.   Season the Watermelon Salsa with kosher salt and black pepper.

5.   Gently toss all the ingredients together until they are well combined.

6.   Taste the salsa and adjust the level of sweetness, spiciness, acidity, or seasoning by adding more honey, jalapeño, lime juice, salt, or pepper as needed.

7.   Let the Watermelon Salsa sit at room temperature for about 15-30 minutes before serving to allow the flavors to meld together. You can also refrigerate it for later use.

Suggested Uses for Watermelon Salsa:

1.   Chips and Dip: Serve it as a refreshing dip for tortilla chips, pita chips, or cinnamon chips.

2.   Grilled Chicken or Shrimp Topping: Spoon it over grilled chicken or shrimp for a tropical and fruity twist.

3.   Taco Filling: Use Watermelon Salsa as a unique and juicy filling for soft tacos or fish tacos.

4.   Summer Salad: Add it to a salad for a sweet and tangy element, or serve it alongside a green salad for a burst of freshness.

5.   Fruit Salsa: Pair it with other fresh fruit, such as mango or pineapple, to create a colorful and flavorful fruit salsa.

Watermelon Salsa is a sweet and refreshing salsa that combines the natural sweetness of watermelon with the crispness of cucumber and the zing of lime juice and spices. It's a delightful and unique condiment that adds a fruity twist to your dishes and is perfect for summer gatherings. Enjoy experimenting with different recipes to showcase the deliciousness of this watermelon salsa.

Chipotle Salsa Recipe

Ingredients:

·   4 ripe tomatoes

·   2 chipotle peppers in adobo sauce (adjust to taste)

·   1/2 white onion, roughly chopped

·   2 cloves garlic, minced

·   1/4 cup fresh cilantro, chopped

·   Juice of 2 limes

·   1/2 teaspoon kosher salt, or to taste

- 1/4 teaspoon black pepper, or to taste
- 1/4 teaspoon ground cumin (optional, for added depth of flavor)

Instructions:

1. Preheat your broiler or grill to high heat.

2. Place the ripe tomatoes on a baking sheet or directly on the grill grates.

3. Roast the tomatoes under the broiler or on the grill until they are charred and blistered, turning them occasionally to ensure even cooking. This will take about 10-15 minutes.

4. Remove the roasted tomatoes from the heat source and let them cool slightly.

5. Once the tomatoes are cool enough to handle, peel the skin off and remove any stems.

6. Combine the roasted tomatoes, chipotle peppers in adobo sauce, roughly chopped white onion, minced garlic, and chopped fresh cilantro in a blender or food processor.

7. Squeeze the juice of 2 limes into the blender or food processor.

8. Season the Chipotle Salsa with kosher salt, black pepper, and ground cumin (if using).

9. Blend the mixture until it reaches your desired salsa consistency. You can make it chunky or smooth, depending on your preference.

10. Taste the salsa and adjust the level of spiciness, acidity, or seasoning by adding more chipotle peppers, lime juice, salt, or pepper as needed.

11. Transfer the Chipotle Salsa to a serving bowl or container. You can serve it immediately or refrigerate it for later use.

Suggested Uses for Chipotle Salsa:

1. Tortilla Chip Dip: Serve it as a smoky and spicy dip for tortilla chips, corn chips, or pita chips.

2. Taco Topping: Use it as a bold and flavorful topping for tacos filled with grilled chicken, beef, shrimp, or vegetables.

3. Grilled Meat Marinade: Use Chipotle Salsa as a marinade or basting sauce for grilled meats like chicken, steak, or pork.

4. Burrito Filling: Include it as a filling for burritos to add a smoky and spicy kick to your meal.

5. Egg Enhancer: Drizzle it over scrambled eggs or omelets for a spicy and flavorful breakfast.

Chipotle Salsa is a smoky and spicy salsa with the distinct flavor of chipotle peppers in adobo sauce. It's known for its bold and robust taste, making it a fantastic condiment to add some heat to your dishes. Enjoy experimenting with different recipes to showcase the deliciousness of this chipotle salsa.

Vinaigrettes

Balsamic Vinaigrette Recipe

Ingredients:

- 1/4 cup balsamic vinegar
- 1/2 cup extra virgin olive oil
- 1 clove garlic, minced (optional)
- 1 teaspoon Dijon mustard (optional for added flavor and emulsification)
- 1 teaspoon honey or maple syrup (optional for sweetness)
- Salt and pepper to taste

Instructions:

1. In a small mixing bowl, combine the balsamic vinegar and minced garlic (if using). If you prefer a smoother vinaigrette, you can use a small food processor or blender to emulsify the ingredients.

2. If you're using Dijon mustard and honey or maple syrup, add them to the bowl.

3. While whisking the mixture (or blending it if using a food processor or blender), slowly drizzle in the extra virgin olive oil. This gradual addition helps emulsify the vinaigrette, creating a creamy texture.

4. Continue whisking or blending until the vinaigrette is well combined, smooth, and slightly thickened.

5. Season the Balsamic Vinaigrette with salt and pepper to taste. Start with a pinch of each and adjust to your preferred level of seasoning.

6. Taste the vinaigrette and adjust the sweetness, acidity, or seasoning by adding more honey or maple syrup, balsamic vinegar, salt, or pepper as needed.

7. Once the vinaigrette is well-balanced and seasoned to your liking, transfer it to a serving container or a glass jar with a lid for storage.

8. You can use the Balsamic Vinaigrette immediately, but it's often even better if allowed to meld the flavors for at least 30 minutes. Store any leftover vinaigrette in the refrigerator.

Suggested Uses for Balsamic Vinaigrette:

1. Salad Dressing: Drizzle it over your favorite salads, whether they include mixed greens, tomatoes, cucumbers, or roasted vegetables.

2. Marinade: Use it as a marinade for grilled chicken, steak, or vegetables to add depth of flavor.

3. Roasted Vegetables: Toss it with roasted vegetables before or after baking for a burst of tangy flavor.

4. Caprese Salad: Use it in a classic Caprese salad with fresh tomatoes, mozzarella, basil, and a sprinkle of salt.

5. Grilled Fruit: Brush it onto grilled fruits like peaches or strawberries to enhance their sweetness and add a hint of acidity.

Balsamic Vinaigrette is a classic and versatile dressing that balances sweetness and tanginess to your dishes. It's easy to make at home and can be customized to your taste preferences. Enjoy experimenting with different recipes to showcase the deliciousness of this balsamic vinaigrette.

Lemon Dijon Vinaigrette Recipe

Ingredients:

- 1/4 cup fresh lemon juice (about 2 lemons)
- 1/2 cup extra virgin olive oil
- 1 clove garlic, minced
- 2 teaspoons Dijon mustard
- 1 teaspoon honey (optional, for sweetness)
- Salt and black pepper to taste

Instructions:

1. Combine the fresh lemon juice and minced garlic in a small mixing bowl.

2. Add the Dijon mustard to the bowl.

3. If you prefer a slightly sweet vinaigrette, add 1 teaspoon of honey (adjust to taste).

4. While whisking the mixture, slowly drizzle in the extra virgin olive oil. This gradual addition helps emulsify the vinaigrette, creating a creamy texture.

5. Continue whisking until the Lemon Dijon Vinaigrette is well combined, smooth, and slightly thickened.

6. Season the vinaigrette with salt and black pepper to taste. Start with a pinch of each and adjust to your preferred level of seasoning.

7. Taste the vinaigrette and adjust the sweetness, acidity, or seasoning by adding more honey, lemon juice, salt, or pepper as needed.

8. Once the vinaigrette is well-balanced and seasoned to your liking, transfer it to a serving container or a glass jar with a lid for storage.

9. You can use the Lemon Dijon Vinaigrette immediately, but it's often even better if allowed to sit for at least 30 minutes to meld the flavors. Store any leftover vinaigrette in the refrigerator.

Suggested Uses for Lemon Dijon Vinaigrette:

1. Salad Dressing: Drizzle it over mixed green salads, spinach salads, or salads with grilled chicken or shrimp.

2. Marinade: Use it as a marinade for chicken, fish, or tofu before grilling or roasting.

3. Roasted Vegetables: Toss it with roasted vegetables for added flavor and brightness.

4.   Grain or Pasta Salad: Mix it into grain salads or pasta salads to infuse them with a zesty kick.

5.   Drizzle for Grilled Meats: Use it as a finishing drizzle for grilled steaks, lamb chops, or pork tenderloin.

Lemon Dijon Vinaigrette is a tangy and flavorful dressing that combines the brightness of fresh lemon juice with the depth of Dijon mustard. It's a versatile vinaigrette that adds a burst of flavor to your dishes and pairs well with salads, grilled meats, and roasted vegetables. Enjoy experimenting with different recipes to showcase the deliciousness of this lemon Dijon vinaigrette.

Honey Mustard Vinaigrette Recipe

Ingredients:

·   1/4 cup Dijon mustard

·   2 tablespoons honey

·   3 tablespoons apple cider vinegar

·   1/4 cup extra virgin olive oil

·   Salt and black pepper to taste

Instructions:

1.   In a small mixing bowl, combine the Dijon mustard and honey.

2.   Add the apple cider vinegar to the bowl and whisk the mixture together until it's well combined.

3.   While whisking, slowly drizzle in the extra virgin olive oil. This gradual addition helps emulsify the vinaigrette, creating a creamy texture.

4.   Continue whisking until the Honey Mustard Vinaigrette is well combined and slightly thickened.

5.   Season the vinaigrette with salt and black pepper to taste. Start with a pinch of each and adjust to your preferred level of seasoning.

6.   Taste the vinaigrette and adjust the sweetness, acidity, or seasoning by adding more honey, apple cider vinegar, salt, or pepper as needed.

7.   Once the vinaigrette is well-balanced and seasoned to your liking, transfer it to a serving container or a glass jar with a lid for storage.

8.   You can use the Honey Mustard Vinaigrette immediately, but it's often even better if allowed to meld the flavors for at least 30 minutes. Store any leftover vinaigrette in the refrigerator.

Suggested Uses for Honey Mustard Vinaigrette:

1.   Salad Dressing: Drizzle it over mixed green salads, spinach salads, or salads with grilled chicken or turkey.

2.   Marinade: Use it as a marinade for chicken breasts, pork chops, or salmon before grilling or baking.

3.   Sandwich Spread: Spread it on sandwiches, wraps, or burgers for added flavor and creaminess.

4.   Dipping Sauce: Serve it as a dip for chicken tenders, pretzel bites, or vegetable sticks.

5.   Glaze for Roasted Vegetables: Toss roasted vegetables in the vinaigrette before serving to add a sweet, tangy glaze.

Honey Mustard Vinaigrette is a classic and versatile dressing that balances the sweetness of honey with the tanginess of Dijon mustard. It's a delicious condiment that can be used in various ways to enhance the flavor of your dishes. Enjoy experimenting with different recipes to showcase the deliciousness of this honey mustard vinaigrette.

Raspberry Vinaigrette Recipe

Ingredients:

·   1/2 cup fresh raspberries

·   1/4 cup extra virgin olive oil

·   2 tablespoons red wine vinegar

·   1 tablespoon honey (adjust to taste)

·   1/4 teaspoon Dijon mustard (optional for added flavor and emulsification)

·   Salt and black pepper to taste

Instructions:

1.   In a small mixing bowl, add the fresh raspberries. Mash them with a fork or the back of a spoon until they are well mashed and have released their juices.

2.   Add the red wine vinegar to the mashed raspberries and stir to combine.

3.   If you're using Dijon mustard and honey, add them to the bowl and mix well.

4.   Slowly drizzle in the extra virgin olive oil while whisking the mixture. This gradual addition helps emulsify the vinaigrette, creating a creamy texture.

5.   Continue whisking until the Raspberry Vinaigrette is well combined and slightly thickened.

6.   Season the vinaigrette with salt and black pepper to taste. Start with a pinch of each and adjust to your preferred level of seasoning.

7.   Taste the vinaigrette and adjust the sweetness, acidity, or seasoning by adding more honey, red wine vinegar, salt, or pepper as needed.

8.   Once the vinaigrette is well-balanced and seasoned to your liking, transfer it to a serving container or a glass jar with a lid for storage.

9.   You can use the Raspberry Vinaigrette immediately, but it's often even better if allowed to meld the flavors for at least 30 minutes. Store any leftover vinaigrette in the refrigerator.

Suggested Uses for Raspberry Vinaigrette:

1.   Salad Dressing: Drizzle it over mixed green salads, spinach salads, or salads with goat cheese, candied nuts, and fresh berries.

2.   Marinade: Use it as a marinade for grilled chicken or shrimp for a fruity and tangy flavor.

3.   Fruit Salad Dressing: Toss it with fresh fruit like strawberries, blueber- ries, and melons for a delightful fruit salad.

4.   Grilled Vegetables: Brush it onto grilled vegetables for a sweet and tangy glaze.

5.   Drizzle for Desserts: Use it as a drizzle over vanilla ice cream, cheesecake, or angel food cake for a fruity dessert.

Raspberry Vinaigrette is a sweet and tangy dressing that combines the vibrant flavor of fresh raspberries with the acidity of red wine vinegar. It's a delightful condiment that adds a burst of fruity freshness to your dishes. Enjoy experimenting with different recipes to showcase the deliciousness of this raspberry vinaigrette.

Italian Vinaigrette Recipe

Ingredients:

·   1/4 cup red wine vinegar

·   1/2 cup extra virgin olive oil

·   1 clove garlic, minced

·   1 teaspoon Dijon mustard

·   1 teaspoon honey or maple syrup (optional for sweetness)

·   1 teaspoon dried oregano

·   1/2 teaspoon dried basil

·   1/2 teaspoon dried thyme

·   Salt and black pepper to taste

Instructions:

1.   Combine the red wine vinegar and minced garlic in a small mixing bowl.

2.   Add the Dijon mustard to the bowl and whisk the mixture together until it's well combined.

3.   If you prefer a slightly sweet vinaigrette, add 1 teaspoon of honey or maple syrup (adjust to taste).

4.   Sprinkle in the dried oregano, dried basil, and dried thyme. These herbs will infuse the vinaigrette with Italian flavors.

5.   Season the Italian Vinaigrette with salt and black pepper to taste. Start with a pinch of each and adjust to your preferred level of seasoning.

6.   Whisk the mixture to combine all the ingredients.

7.   Slowly drizzle in the extra virgin olive oil while whisking the vinaigrette. This gradual addition helps emulsify the vinaigrette, creating a creamy texture.

8.   Continue whisking until the vinaigrette is well combined and slightly thickened.

9.   Taste the vinaigrette and adjust the sweetness, acidity, or seasoning by adding more honey, red wine vinegar, salt, or pepper as needed.

10.   Once the Italian Vinaigrette is well-balanced and seasoned to your liking, transfer it to a serving container or a glass jar with a lid for storage.

11.   You can use the vinaigrette immediately, but it's often even better if allowed to sit for at least 30 minutes to meld the flavors. Store any leftover vinaigrette in the refrigerator.

Suggested Uses for Italian Vinaigrette:

1.   Salad Dressing: Drizzle it over classic Italian salads like Caprese salad or dress mixed greens with tomatoes, olives, and fresh mozzarella.

2.   Marinade: Use it as a marinade for grilled chicken, beef, or vegetables to infuse them with Italian flavors.

3.   Pasta Salad: Toss it with cooked pasta, cherry tomatoes, cucumbers, and feta cheese for a flavorful pasta salad.

4.   Bruschetta Topping: Spoon it over toasted baguette slices for a quick and delicious bruschetta.

5.   Grilled Vegetables: Brush it onto grilled vegetables for an Italian- inspired side dish.

Italian Vinaigrette is a classic dressing that captures the flavors of Italy with herbs and seasonings. It's a versatile condiment that adds Mediterranean flair to your dishes. Enjoy experimenting with different recipes to showcase the deliciousness of this Italian vinaigrette.

Cilantro Lime Vinaigrette Recipe

Ingredients:

- 1/4 cup fresh lime juice (about 2-3 limes)
- 1/2 cup extra virgin olive oil
- 1/4 cup fresh cilantro leaves, chopped
- 2 cloves garlic, minced
- 1 teaspoon honey or maple syrup (optional, for sweetness)
- Salt and black pepper to taste

Instructions:

1.   Combine the fresh lime juice and minced garlic in a small mixing bowl.

2.   If you prefer a slightly sweet vinaigrette, add 1 teaspoon of honey or maple syrup (adjust to taste).

3.   Sprinkle in the freshly chopped cilantro leaves.

4.   Season the Cilantro Lime Vinaigrette with salt and black pepper to taste. Start with a pinch of each and adjust to your preferred level of seasoning.

5.   Whisk the mixture together to combine all the ingredients.

6.   While whisking, slowly drizzle in the extra virgin olive oil. This gradual addition helps emulsify the vinaigrette, creating a creamy texture.

7.   Continue whisking until the vinaigrette is well combined and slightly thickened.

8.   Taste the vinaigrette and adjust the sweetness, acidity, or seasoning by adding more honey, lime juice, salt, or pepper as needed.

9.   Once the Cilantro Lime Vinaigrette is well-balanced and seasoned to your liking, transfer it to a serving container or a glass jar with a lid for storage.

10.   You can use the vinaigrette immediately, but it's often even better if allowed to sit for at least 30 minutes to meld the flavors. Store any leftover vinaigrette in the refrigerator.

Suggested Uses for Cilantro Lime Vinaigrette:

1.   Salad Dressing: Drizzle it over salads with mixed greens, avocado, tomatoes, and grilled chicken or shrimp.

2.   Grilled Meats: Use it as a marinade for grilled meats such as chicken, steak, or pork.

3.   Fish Topping: Spoon it over grilled or baked fish for a burst of fresh flavor.

4.   Taco Sauce: Use it as a sauce for tacos, including fish tacos or shrimp tacos.

5.   Cilantro Lime Rice: Mix it into cooked rice for a zesty and aromatic side dish.

Cilantro Lime Vinaigrette is a zesty and vibrant dressing that combines the bright citrusy flavor of lime with the freshness of cilantro. It's a versatile condiment that adds a burst of flavor to your dishes and pairs well with salads, grilled meats, and seafood. Enjoy experimenting with different recipes to showcase the deliciousness of this cilantro lime vinaigrette.

Greek Salad Dressing Recipe

Ingredients:
- 1/4 cup red wine vinegar
- 1/2 cup extra virgin olive oil
- 1 teaspoon dried oregano
- 1 teaspoon dried basil

- 1 clove garlic, minced

- 1/2 teaspoon Dijon mustard (optional for added flavor and emulsification)

- Salt and black pepper to taste

Instructions:

1.	Combine the red wine vinegar and minced garlic in a small mixing bowl.

2.	If you prefer a slightly creamy texture and added flavor, add 1/2 teaspoon of Dijon mustard (adjust to taste).

3.	Sprinkle in the dried oregano and dried basil. These herbs will infuse the dressing with Mediterranean flavors.

4.	Season the Greek Salad Dressing with salt and black pepper to taste. Start with a pinch of each and adjust to your preferred level of seasoning.

5.	Whisk the mixture together to combine all the ingredients.

6.	While whisking, slowly drizzle in the extra virgin olive oil. This gradual addition helps emulsify the dressing, creating a creamy texture.

7.	Continue whisking until the Greek Salad Dressing is well combined and slightly thickened.

8.	Taste the dressing and adjust the seasoning or herb flavors by adding more salt, pepper, oregano, or basil as needed.

9.	Once the dressing is well-balanced and seasoned to your liking, transfer it to a serving container or a glass jar with a lid for storage.

10.	You can use the Greek Salad Dressing immediately, but it's often even better if allowed to sit for at least 30 minutes to meld the flavors. Store any leftover dressing in the refrigerator.

Suggested Uses for Greek Salad Dressing:

1.	Greek Salad: Toss it with a classic Greek salad made with cucumbers, tomatoes, red onions, Kalamata olives, feta cheese, and lettuce or spinach.

2.	Marinade: Use it as a marinade for grilled chicken, lamb, or shrimp to infuse them with Mediterranean flavors.

3.	Pasta Salad: Mix it into a pasta salad with colorful bell peppers, cherry tomatoes, and feta cheese.

4.	Vegetable Dip: Serve it as a dip for fresh vegetable sticks like cucumbers, carrots, and bell peppers.

5.	Roasted Vegetables: Drizzle it over roasted vegetables like zucchini, eggplant, and red bell peppers for extra flavor.

Greek Salad Dressing is a flavorful dressing that captures the essence of Mediterranean cuisine with herbs, garlic, and red wine vinegar. It's a versatile condiment that adds a delightful Mediterranean touch to your salads and dishes. Enjoy experimenting with different recipes to showcase the deliciousness of this Greek salad dressing.

Sesame Ginger Vinaigrette Recipe

Ingredients:

- · 1/4 cup rice vinegar
- · 2 tablespoons soy sauce
- · 1 tablespoon sesame oil
- · 1 tablespoon fresh ginger, grated
- · 1 clove garlic, minced
- · 1 teaspoon honey or maple syrup (optional, for sweetness)
- · 1/4 cup vegetable or canola oil
- · 1 tablespoon sesame seeds (optional, for garnish)
- · Salt and black pepper to taste

Instructions:

1. In a small mixing bowl, combine the rice vinegar and soy sauce.

2. Add the sesame oil to the bowl and whisk the mixture together.

3. Grate fresh ginger into the bowl. You can use a fine grater or a zester for this.

4. Add minced garlic to the bowl and mix well.

5. If you prefer a slightly sweet vinaigrette, add 1 teaspoon of honey or maple syrup (adjust to taste).

6. Season the Sesame Ginger Vinaigrette with salt and black pepper to taste. Start with a pinch of each and adjust to your preferred level of seasoning.

7. While whisking, slowly drizzle in the vegetable or canola oil. This gradual addition helps emulsify the vinaigrette, creating a creamy texture.

8. Continue whisking until the vinaigrette is well combined and slightly thickened.

9. Taste the vinaigrette and adjust the sweetness, acidity, or seasoning by adding more honey, rice vinegar, salt, or pepper as needed.

10. Once the Sesame Ginger Vinaigrette is well-balanced and seasoned to your liking, transfer it to a serving container or a glass jar with a lid for storage.

11. If desired, sprinkle sesame seeds over the vinaigrette for garnish.

12. You can use the vinaigrette immediately, but it's often even better if allowed to sit for at least 30 minutes to meld the flavors. Store any leftover vinaigrette in the refrigerator.

Suggested Uses for Sesame Ginger Vinaigrette:

1. Salad Dressing: Drizzle it over Asian-inspired salads with mixed greens, mandarin oranges, crispy wonton strips, and grilled chicken or tofu.

2. Marinade: Use it as a marinade for chicken, shrimp, or salmon before grilling or stir-frying.

3. Stir-Fry Sauce: Add it to stir-fried vegetables and protein for a flavorful stir-fry.

4. Noodle Salad: Toss it with cold noodles, vegetables, and herbs for a refreshing noodle salad.

5. Drizzle for Grilled Vegetables: Use it to brush grilled vegetables like asparagus or bell peppers for an Asian twist.

Sesame Ginger Vinaigrette is a zesty and aromatic dressing that combines the nuttiness of sesame oil with the freshness of ginger and the umami of soy sauce. It's a versatile condiment that adds a burst of Asian-inspired flavor to your dishes. Enjoy experimenting with different recipes to showcase the deliciousness of this sesame ginger vinaigrette.

Caesar Dressing Recipe

Ingredients:

· 1/2 cup mayonnaise

· 2 cloves garlic, minced

· 2 tablespoons grated Parmesan cheese

· 1 1/2 tablespoons lemon juice

· 1 teaspoon Dijon mustard

· 1/2 teaspoon Worcestershire sauce

· 1/2 teaspoon anchovy paste (optional, for traditional Caesar flavor)

· Salt and black pepper to taste

Instructions:

1. In a small mixing bowl, combine the mayonnaise and minced garlic.

2. Add the grated Parmesan cheese to the bowl and mix it in.

3. Squeeze fresh lemon juice into the mixture and stir well.

4. Stir in the Dijon mustard and Worcestershire sauce.

5. If you want to achieve the traditional Caesar flavor, you can add 1/2 teaspoon of anchovy paste to the dressing at this point. (Optional)

6. Season the Caesar Dressing with salt and black pepper to taste. Start with a pinch of each and adjust to your preferred level of seasoning.

7. Stir all the ingredients together until the dressing is well combined and creamy.

8. Taste the dressing and adjust the acidity or seasoning by adding more lemon juice, salt, or pepper as needed.

9. Once the Caesar Dressing is well-balanced and seasoned to your liking, transfer it to a serving container or a glass jar with a lid for storage.

10. You can use the dressing immediately, but it's often even better if allowed to sit for at least 30 minutes to meld the flavors. Store any leftover dressing in the refrigerator.

Suggested Uses for Caesar Dressing:

1.   Classic Caesar Salad: Toss it with romaine lettuce, croutons, and additional grated Parmesan cheese for a classic Caesar salad.

2.   Chicken Caesar Salad: Drizzle it over a salad with grilled chicken strips for a hearty meal.

3.   Caesar Wrap: Spread it on tortillas or flatbreads, add grilled chicken or shrimp, lettuce, and roll into a wrap.

4.   Vegetable Dip: Use it as a dip for fresh vegetable sticks like celery and carrots.

5.   Potato Salad: Mix it into potato salad for a creamy and tangy twist.

Caesar Dressing is a creamy and savory dressing that's known for its bold flavors. It's a classic condiment that adds a rich and tangy kick to your salads and other dishes. Enjoy the versatility of this Caesar dressing in various recipes.

Blue Cheese Vinaigrette Recipe

Ingredients:

·   1/4 cup red wine vinegar

·   1/2 cup extra virgin olive oil

·   1/3 cup crumbled blue cheese

·   1 clove garlic, minced

·   1 teaspoon Dijon mustard

·   1 teaspoon honey or maple syrup (optional, for sweetness)

·   Salt and black pepper to taste

Instructions:

1.   Combine the red wine vinegar and minced garlic in a small mixing bowl.

2.   Add the Dijon mustard to the bowl and whisk the mixture together until it's well combined.

3.   If you prefer a slightly sweet vinaigrette, add 1 teaspoon of honey or maple syrup (adjust to taste).

4.   Sprinkle in the crumbled blue cheese. You can use a fork to break up larger chunks if necessary.

5.   Season the Blue Cheese Vinaigrette with salt and black pepper to taste. Start with a pinch of each and adjust to your preferred level of seasoning.

6.   Whisk the mixture to combine all the ingredients.

7.   While whisking, slowly drizzle in the extra virgin olive oil. This gradual addition helps emulsify the vinaigrette, creating a creamy texture.

8.   Continue whisking until the vinaigrette is well combined and slightly thickened.

9.   Taste the vinaigrette and adjust the sweetness, acidity, or seasoning by adding more honey, red wine vinegar, salt, or pepper as needed.

10.   Once the Blue Cheese Vinaigrette is well-balanced and seasoned to your liking, transfer it to a serving container or a glass jar with a lid for storage.

11.   You can use the vinaigrette immediately, but it's often even better if allowed to sit for at least 30 minutes to meld the flavors. Store any leftover vinaigrette in the refrigerator.

Suggested Uses for Blue Cheese Vinaigrette:

1.   Salad Dressing: Drizzle it over salads with mixed greens, chopped walnuts, sliced pears, and additional crumbled blue cheese.

2.   Steak Salad: Use it as a dressing for a hearty steak salad with grilled steak slices, cherry tomatoes, and mixed greens.

3.   Burger Topping: Spread it on burgers for a rich and tangy flavor.

4.   Wing Dip: Serve it as a dip for chicken wings or cauliflower wings.

5.   Vegetable Dip: Use it as a dip for fresh vegetable sticks like celery and carrots.

Blue Cheese Vinaigrette is a creamy and tangy dressing that's perfect for those who love the bold flavor of blue cheese. It's a versatile condiment that adds richness to salads and pairs well with grilled meats. Enjoy experimenting with different recipes to showcase the deliciousness of this blue cheese vinaigrette.

Balsamic Reduction Recipe

Ingredients:

- 1 cup balsamic vinegar
- 2 tablespoons brown sugar (optional, for sweetness)

Instructions:

1.   In a small saucepan, combine 1 cup of balsamic vinegar and, if desired, 2 tablespoons of brown sugar for sweetness. The sugar is optional, and you can adjust the amount to your taste.

2.   Place the saucepan over medium heat and bring the balsamic vinegar to a gentle boil.

3.   Reduce the heat to low to maintain a simmer. Allow the vinegar to simmer gently for approximately 15-20 minutes, or until it has thickened and reduced by half. Stir occasionally to prevent sticking and burning.

4.   Keep a close eye on the reduction as it nears completion to prevent over- thickening or burning. The reduction is ready when it coats the back of a spoon and has a syrup-like consistency.

5.   Remove the saucepan from the heat and let the balsamic reduction cool to room temperature. It will continue to thicken as it cools.

6.   Once cooled, transfer the balsamic reduction to an airtight container or a glass bottle with a tight-sealing lid. Store it in the refrigerator.

Suggested uses

1.   Caprese Salad Drizzle: Add a touch of balsamic reduction to your Caprese salad made with fresh tomatoes, mozzarella, basil, and olive oil.

2.   Glaze for Grilled Chicken: Brush balsamic reduction over grilled chicken breasts during the last few minutes of cooking for a sweet, tangy glaze.

3.   Roasted Vegetable Enhancer: Drizzle balsamic reduction over roasted vegetables like asparagus, Brussels sprouts, or carrots to elevate their flavor.

4.   Strawberry Balsamic Dessert: Serve fresh strawberries drizzled with balsamic reduction and a scoop of vanilla ice cream for a delightful dessert.

5.   Marinade for Pork or Beef: Use balsamic reduction as a marinade for pork chops or beef steaks before grilling or pan-searing to infuse them with rich flavor.

Red Wine Reduction Recipe

Ingredients:

- ·   1 cup red wine (choose a good-quality wine you enjoy)

- ·   1/4 cup finely chopped shallots

- ·   2 cloves garlic, minced

- ·   1 cup beef or vegetable broth

- ·   2 tablespoons unsalted butter

- ·   Salt and black pepper to taste

Instructions:

1.   In a saucepan, sauté the finely chopped shallots in 1 tablespoon of butter over medium heat until they become translucent, about 2-3 minutes.

2.   Add the minced garlic to the shallots and sauté for another 30 seconds, or until fragrant.

3.   Pour in 1 cup of red wine and bring it to a simmer. Allow it to reduce by half, which should take about 15-20 minutes. Stir occasionally.

4.   Once the wine has reduced, add 1 cup of beef or vegetable broth. Continue to simmer until the mixture reduces by half again and thickens, which should take about 15-20 more minutes.

5.   Remove the saucepan from the heat and whisk in the remaining 1 tablespoon of butter until the sauce is glossy. Season with salt and black pepper to taste.

6.   Strain the red wine reduction through a fine-mesh sieve into a serving dish or container to remove any solids.

7.   Serve the red wine reduction immediately or store it in the refrigerator for later use.

Suggested Uses for Red Wine Reduction:

1.   Filet Mignon Sauce: Pour the red wine reduction over grilled or pan- seared filet mignon steaks for a luxurious and flavorful sauce.

2.   Duck Breast Glaze: To enhance their richness, use the reduction as a glaze for roasted or pan-seared duck breasts.

3.   Lamb Chops Drizzle: Drizzle the red wine reduction over grilled lamb chops for a sophisticated touch.

4.   Mushroom Risotto Enhancer: Stir the reduction into a creamy mush- room risotto for depth of flavor.

5.   Portobello Burger Topping: Spoon the red wine reduction onto grilled Portobello mushroom caps when assembling veggie burgers for a gourmet twist.

This versatile red wine reduction adds a rich and savory element to a variety of dishes, making them even more delicious and elegant.

Reductions

Port Wine Reduction Recipe

Ingredients:

·   1 cup port wine

·   1/4 cup finely chopped shallots

·   2 cloves garlic, minced

·   1 cup beef or vegetable broth

·   2 tablespoons unsalted butter

·   Salt and black pepper to taste

Instructions:

1.   In a saucepan, sauté the finely chopped shallots in 1 tablespoon of butter over medium heat until they become translucent, about 2-3 minutes.

2.   Add the minced garlic to the shallots and sauté for another 30 seconds, or until fragrant.

3.   Pour in 1 cup of port wine and bring it to a simmer. Allow it to reduce by half, which should take about 15-20 minutes. Stir occasionally.

4.   Once the port wine has reduced, add 1 cup of beef or vegetable broth. Continue to simmer until the mixture reduces by half again and thickens, which should take about 15-20 more minutes.

5.   Remove the saucepan from the heat and whisk in the remaining 1 tablespoon of butter until the sauce is glossy. Season with salt and black pepper to taste.

6.   Strain the port wine reduction through a fine-mesh sieve into a serving dish or container to remove any solids.

7.   Serve the port wine reduction immediately or store it in the refrigerator for later use.

Suggested Uses for Port Wine Reduction:

1.   Steak Enhancement: Drizzle the port wine reduction over grilled or pan-seared steaks, such as ribeye or sirloin, for a luxurious and flavorful sauce.

2.   Chicken Liver Pâté: Incorporate the reduction into chicken liver pâté for a rich and velvety spread.

3.   Roasted Game Meat Glaze: Use the reduction as a glaze for roasted game meats like venison or duck to complement their bold flavors.

4.   Blue Cheese Crostini: Spoon the port wine reduction over blue cheese crostini for an elegant appetizer.

5.   Roasted Vegetable Medley: Toss roasted vegetables in the reduction before serving to add a touch of sophistication to the dish.

This luscious port wine reduction brings depth and elegance to a variety of dishes, from meats to appetizers and side dishes.

Port Wine Reduction Recipe

Ingredients:

- · 1 cup port wine

- · 1/4 cup finely chopped shallots

- · 2 cloves garlic, minced

- · 1 cup beef or vegetable broth

- · 2 tablespoons unsalted butter

- · Salt and black pepper to taste

Instructions:

1.   In a saucepan, sauté the finely chopped shallots in 1 tablespoon of butter over medium heat until they become translucent, about 2-3 minutes.

2.   Add the minced garlic to the shallots and sauté for another 30 seconds, or until fragrant.

3.   Pour in 1 cup of port wine and bring it to a simmer. Allow it to reduce by half, which should take about 15-20 minutes. Stir occasionally.

4.   Once the port wine has reduced, add 1 cup of beef or vegetable broth. Continue to simmer until the mixture reduces by

half again and thickens, which should take about 15-20 more minutes.

5.   Remove the saucepan from the heat and whisk in the remaining 1 tablespoon of butter until the sauce is glossy. Season with salt and black pepper to taste.

6.   Strain the port wine reduction through a fine-mesh sieve into a serving dish or container to remove any solids.

7.   Serve the port wine reduction immediately or store it in the refrigerator for later use.

Suggested Uses for Port Wine Reduction:

1.   Steak Enhancement: Drizzle the port wine reduction over grilled or pan- seared steaks, such as ribeye or sirloin, for a luxurious and flavorful sauce.

2.   Chicken Liver Pâté: Incorporate the reduction into chicken liver pâté for a rich and velvety spread.

3.   Roasted Game Meat Glaze: Use the reduction as a glaze for roasted game meats like venison or duck to complement their bold flavors.

4.   Blue Cheese Crostini: Spoon the port wine reduction over blue cheese crostini for an elegant appetizer.

5.   Roasted Vegetable Medley: Toss roasted vegetables in the reduction before serving to add a touch of sophistication to the dish.

This luscious port wine reduction brings depth and elegance to a variety of dishes, from meats to appetizers and side dishes.

Maple Syrup Reduction Recipe:

Ingredients:

- 1 cup pure maple syrup
- 1/4 cup water
- 1 cinnamon stick (optional)
- 2-3 whole cloves (optional)
- 1/2 teaspoon vanilla extract (optional)

Instructions:

1.   Combine 1 cup of pure maple syrup in a small saucepan and 1/4 cup of water. If desired, add a cinnamon stick, whole cloves, or vanilla extract for extra flavor.

2.   Place the saucepan over medium heat and bring the mixture to a simmer.

3.   Reduce the heat to low to maintain a gentle simmer. Allow the mixture to simmer for about 15-20 minutes, or until it has thickened and reduced by about half. Stir occasionally.

4.   Keep a close eye on the reduction to ensure it doesn't over-thicken or burn. It should have a syrupy consistency when done.

5.   Remove the saucepan from the heat and let the maple syrup reduction cool. If you added spices or vanilla extract, you can strain them out at this point, or leave them in for added flavor.

6.   Once cooled, transfer the maple syrup reduction to an airtight container or bottle with a tight-sealing lid.

Suggested Uses for Maple Syrup Reduction:

1.   Pancake and Waffle Drizzle: Pour the maple syrup reduction over pancakes, waffles, or French toast for a rich and flavorful topping.

2.   Glaze for Roasted Vegetables: Use the reduction as a glaze for roasted root vegetables like carrots, sweet potatoes, and parsnips.

3.   Maple-Glazed Salmon: Brush the reduction onto salmon fillets before baking or grilling for a sweet and savory glaze.

4.   Dessert Enhancer: Drizzle the reduction over vanilla ice cream, cheese- cake, or apple pie for a decadent dessert.

5.   Salad Dressing Component: Incorporate the maple syrup reduction into salad dressings for a touch of sweetness and complexity.

This homemade maple syrup reduction adds a delightful sweetness and depth of flavor to a variety of dishes, from breakfast to dessert and everything in between.

Fig Reduction Recipe

Ingredients:

·   1 cup fresh figs, stemmed and quartered

·   1/2 cup water

·   1/4 cup granulated sugar

·   1 tablespoon lemon juice

·   Pinch of salt

Instructions:

1.   Combine the fresh figs, water, granulated sugar, lemon juice, and a pinch of salt in a saucepan.

2.   Place the saucepan over medium heat and bring the mixture to a simmer, stirring to dissolve the sugar.

3.   Reduce the heat to low to maintain a gentle simmer. Allow the mixture to simmer for about 15-20 minutes, or until the figs have softened and the liquid has thickened to a syrupy consistency. Stir occasionally.

4.   Remove the saucepan from the heat and let the fig reduction cool slightly.

5.   Use an immersion or regular blender to puree the mixture until smooth. Be cautious, as it will be hot.

6.   Once blended, strain the fig reduction through a fine-mesh sieve into a clean container to remove any remaining solids.

7.   Let the fig reduction cool completely before transferring it to an airtight container or bottle with a tight-sealing lid.

Suggested Uses for Fig Reduction:

1.   Cheese Plate Accompaniment: Drizzle the fig reduction over a cheese platter with a variety of cheeses, nuts, and crackers.

2.   Pork Tenderloin Glaze: Use the reduction as a glaze for roasted or grilled pork tenderloin to add sweet and fruity notes.

3.   Fig and Prosciutto Flatbread: Spread the fig reduction on a flatbread or pizza crust and top with prosciutto, arugula, and cheese for a delicious appetizer.

4.   Salad Dressing Component: Incorporate the fig reduction into salad dressings for a unique and fruity twist.

5.   Dessert Topping: Spoon the fig reduction over vanilla ice cream, Greek yogurt, or panna cotta for a delightful dessert topping.

This homemade fig reduction offers a sweet and fruity flavor that pairs well with both savory and sweet dishes, making it a versatile addition to your culinary creations.

Orange Cognac Reduction Recipe

Ingredients:

·   1 cup fresh orange juice (about 4-5 oranges)

·   1/4 cup cognac or brandy

·   1/4 cup granulated sugar

·   Zest of 1 orange

·   1 cinnamon stick (optional)

·   2-3 whole cloves (optional)

Instructions:

1.   In a saucepan, combine 1 cup of fresh orange juice, 1/4 cup of cognac or brandy, 1/4 cup of granulated sugar, the zest of 1 orange, and, if desired, a cinnamon stick and 2-3 whole cloves for added flavor.

2.   Place the saucepan over medium heat and stir to dissolve the sugar.

3.   Bring the mixture to a simmer and then reduce the heat to low to maintain a gentle simmer.

4.   Allow the mixture to simmer for about 15-20 minutes, or until it has thickened and reduced by about half. Stir occasionally.

5.   Remove the saucepan from the heat and let the Orange Cognac Reduction cool slightly. If you added spices, you can strain them out at this point, or leave them in for added flavor.

6.   Once cooled, transfer the reduction to an airtight container or bottle with a tight-sealing lid.

Suggested Uses for Orange Cognac Reduction:

1.   Duck à l'Orange: Use the reduction as a glaze for duck breasts or duck confit for a classic Duck à l'Orange.

2.   Sautéed Shrimp: Drizzle the Orange Cognac Reduction over sautéed shrimp or prawns for a sweet and citrusy sauce.

3.   Pork Medallion Sauce: Serve the reduction as a sauce for pan-seared or grilled pork medallions for a burst of flavor.

4.   Citrusy Desserts: Drizzle it over desserts like cheesecake, pound cake, or crepes to add a tangy-sweet twist.

5.   Fruit Salad Dressing: Incorporate the reduction into the dressing for a fruit salad to enhance its flavor.

This homemade Orange Cognac Reduction brings a delightful blend of orange and brandy flavors, making it an excellent addition to both savory and sweet dishes.

Teriyaki Glaze Recipe

Ingredients:

·   1/2 cup soy sauce

·   1/4 cup mirin (Japanese sweet rice wine)

·   1/4 cup sake (Japanese rice wine) or dry white wine

·   1/4 cup granulated sugar

·   2 cloves garlic, minced

·   1 tablespoon fresh ginger, minced

·   1 tablespoon cornstarch (for thickening)

·   2 tablespoons cold water (for cornstarch slurry)

Instructions:

1.   In a saucepan, combine 1/2 cup of soy sauce, 1/4 cup of mirin, 1/4 cup of sake (or dry white wine), 1/4 cup of granulated sugar, minced garlic, and minced ginger.

2.   Place the saucepan over medium heat and stir until the sugar has dissolved.

3.   In a separate small bowl, mix 1 tablespoon of cornstarch with 2 table- spoons of cold water to create a cornstarch slurry.

4.   Pour the cornstarch slurry into the saucepan with the other ingredients and stir well.

5.   Bring the mixture to a simmer, then reduce the heat to low and let it simmer for about 5-7 minutes, or until the teriyaki glaze thickens and becomes glossy. Stir occasionally.

6.   Remove the saucepan from the heat and let the teriyaki glaze cool to room temperature.

7.   Once cooled, transfer the glaze to an airtight container or bottle with a tight-sealing lid.

Suggested Uses for Teriyaki Glaze:

1.　　　Teriyaki Chicken: Brush the glaze onto grilled or pan-seared chicken for classic teriyaki chicken.

2.　　　Teriyaki Salmon: Glaze salmon fillets with the teriyaki sauce and broil or grill them for a flavorful salmon dish.

3.　　　Teriyaki Stir-Fry: Use the glaze as a sauce for stir-fried vegetables and protein of your choice.

4.　　　Teriyaki Beef Skewers: Marinate beef skewers in the glaze and grill them for tasty teriyaki beef skewers.

5.　　　Teriyaki Noodles: Toss cooked noodles with the glaze, vegetables, and protein for a delicious teriyaki noodle dish.

This homemade Teriyaki Glaze offers a sweet and savory flavor that's perfect for enhancing a variety of dishes, particularly those with Asian-inspired flavors.

Blueberry Reduction Recipe

Ingredients:

- 1 cup fresh or frozen blueberries
- 1/4 cup granulated sugar
- 2 tablespoons lemon juice
- 1/4 cup water

Instructions:

1.　　　In a saucepan, combine 1 cup of fresh or frozen blueberries, 1/4 cup of granulated sugar, 2 tablespoons of lemon juice, and 1/4 cup of water.

2.　　　Place the saucepan over medium heat and stir to dissolve the sugar.

3.　　　Bring the mixture to a simmer and then reduce the heat to low to maintain a gentle simmer.

4.　　　Allow the mixture to simmer for about 15-20 minutes, or until the blueberries have softened and the liquid has thickened to a syrupy consistency. Stir occasionally.

5.　　　If you prefer a smoother texture, you can use an immersion blender or a regular blender to puree the mixture until smooth.

6.　　　Remove the saucepan from the heat and let the Blueberry Reduction cool slightly.

7.　　　Once cooled, transfer the reduction to an airtight container or bottle with a tight-sealing lid.

Suggested Uses for Blueberry Reduction:

1.　　　Pancake and Waffle Drizzle: Drizzle the Blueberry Reduction over pancakes, waffles, or French toast for a fruity and sweet topping.

2.　　　Pork Tenderloin Glaze: Use the reduction as a glaze for roasted or grilled pork tenderloin to add a burst of berry flavor.

3.   Yogurt and Parfait Enhancer: Spoon the reduction over yogurt or use it to layer parfaits for a delightful fruity element.

4.   Dessert Topping: Drizzle the Blueberry Reduction over cheesecake, ice cream, or pound cake for a luscious dessert topping.

5.   Salad Dressing Component: Incorporate the reduction into salad dress- ings to add a fruity twist to your salads.

This homemade Blueberry Reduction brings a burst of fruity flavor that can elevate a wide range of dishes, from breakfast to dessert and beyond.

Rosemary Lemon Reduction Recipe

Ingredients:

·   1 cup fresh lemon juice (about 4-5 lemons)

·   Zest of 2 lemons

·   2-3 sprigs of fresh rosemary

·   1/4 cup granulated sugar

·   1/4 cup water

Instructions:

1.   In a saucepan, combine 1 cup of fresh lemon juice, the zest of 2 lemons, 2-3 sprigs of fresh rosemary, 1/4 cup of granu- lated sugar, and 1/4 cup of water.

2.   Place the saucepan over medium heat and stir to dissolve the sugar.

3.   Bring the mixture to a simmer, and then reduce the heat to low to maintain a gentle simmer.

4.   Allow the mixture to simmer for about 15-20 minutes, or until it has thickened and reduced by about half. Stir occasionally.

5.   Remove the saucepan from the heat and let the Rosemary Lemon Reduction cool slightly.

6.   Once cooled, remove the rosemary sprigs and transfer the reduction to an airtight container or bottle with a tight-sealing lid.

Suggested Uses for Rosemary Lemon Reduction:

1.   Grilled Chicken Glaze: Brush the Rosemary Lemon Reduction onto grilled chicken breasts or thighs for a zesty and aromatic glaze.

2.   Salmon Topping: Spoon the reduction over grilled or baked salmon fillets to enhance their flavor with a citrusy twist.

3.   Roasted Vegetables Drizzle: Drizzle the reduction over roasted vegeta- bles like potatoes or carrots for a refreshing touch.

4.   Salad Dressing Component: Incorporate the reduction into salad dress- ings for a unique and aromatic addition to your salads.

5.   Lamb Chop Finisher: Use the reduction as a finishing sauce for pan- seared or grilled lamb chops for an elegant and herbaceous touch.

This homemade Rosemary Lemon Reduction combines the bright and citrusy notes of lemon with the earthy aroma of rosemary, making it a versatile addition to a variety of savory dishes.

Brown Butter Sage Reduction Recipe

Ingredients:

- 1/2 cup (1 stick) unsalted butter
- 10-12 fresh sage leaves
- 2 cloves garlic, minced (optional)
- Salt and black pepper to taste

Instructions:

1.   In a saucepan, melt 1/2 cup of unsalted butter over medium heat. Continue to cook the butter until it turns a deep golden brown color. This should take about 5-7 minutes. Stir frequently to prevent burning.

2.   As the butter browns, add 10-12 fresh sage leaves to the pan. If desired, you can also add minced garlic at this point for extra flavor.

3.   Continue to cook the butter and sage for an additional 2-3 minutes, allowing the sage leaves to crisp up and infuse the butter with their flavor.

4.   Remove the saucepan from the heat and season the brown butter sage reduction with salt and black pepper to taste.

5.   Remove the crispy sage leaves from the saucepan and set them aside for garnish or snacking.

6.   Serve the Brown Butter Sage Reduction immediately or transfer it to an airtight container.

Suggested Uses for Brown Butter Sage Reduction:

1.   Butternut Squash Ravioli Sauce: Toss cooked butternut squash ravioli in the reduction for a rich and nutty sauce.

2.   Pan-Seared Chicken: Drizzle the reduction over pan-seared chicken breasts or thighs for a savory and aromatic finish.

3.   Gnocchi Sauce: Serve the reduction as a sauce for potato gnocchi, garnished with crispy sage leaves.

4.   Roasted Vegetables: Drizzle the reduction over roasted vegetables like Brussels sprouts, asparagus, or sweet potatoes for added depth of flavor.

5.   Sage Brown Butter Pasta: Toss cooked pasta in the reduction, and top with grated Parmesan cheese and the reserved crispy sage leaves.

This homemade Brown Butter Sage Reduction adds a nutty richness and herbal aroma to various dishes, making it a delightful addition to your culinary creations.

6

Conclusion

In "Rubs, Marinades, and Sauces," we've embarked on a flavorful journey through the world of culinary alchemy. These simple yet powerful concoctions have the ability to transform ordinary ingredients into extraordinary meals, elevating your cooking from mundane to magnificent.

Throughout this book, we've explored various rubs, marinades, and sauces, each with its unique blend of flavors and aromas. From the smoky depths of barbecue rubs, the zesty freshness of citrus marinades, and the creamy richness of classic sauces, your culinary repertoire has expanded beyond measure.

As you've ventured into the art of seasoning and flavor enhancement, you've discovered that it's not just about the ingredients but the stories, traditions, and memories that each rub, marinade, or sauce can evoke. The sizzle of the grill, the comforting aroma of a slow-cooked stew, or the zing of a perfectly balanced vinaigrette—it's all part of the experience.

With every recipe, you've unlocked the secrets of flavor layering, under- standing the harmonious dance between sweet and savory, spicy and mild, tangy and rich. You've learned that a well-chosen rub can create a flavorful crust on a steak, a marinade can tenderize and infuse the meat with depth, and a sauce can tie it all together in a luscious embrace.

But this journey doesn't end here. The world of culinary creativity is boundless, and your kitchen is a canvas waiting for your inspired brush strokes. Experiment, tweak, and personalize these recipes to suit your taste. Let your taste buds guide you, and don't be afraid to embark on new flavor adventures. Whether you're grilling up a feast for friends, simmering a comforting stew for family, or simply indulging in the pleasure of a well-seasoned dish on a quiet evening, the knowledge and skills you've gained from "Rubs, Marinades,

and Sauces" will continue to enrich your culinary endeavors.

So, as you savor the last pages of this book, remember that the world of flavors is yours to explore. You can turn any meal into a masterpiece with a dash of creativity and a sprinkle of passion. Here's to many more delicious adventures in your kitchen—may they be seasoned to perfection and savored with joy.

Thank you for choosing our recipes and allowing us to assist you in creating delightful dishes. We hope you've enjoyed preparing and savoring these culinary creations as much as we enjoyed providing you with the recipes. Your satisfaction is important to us, and we would greatly appreciate it if you could take a moment to leave a review. Your feedback helps us continually improve and offer you even better assistance in the future. Thank you once again for choosing our services, and we look forward to hearing your thoughts!

www.ingramcontent.com/pod-product-compliance
Lightning Source LLC
Chambersburg PA
CBHW082146120626
46553CB00010B/2792